ISSUE 02 2018/19

WOODSKILLS

The semiannual magazine for the discerning, modern fine woodworking enthusiast

Furniture Maker Edition

STUDY WOODWORKERS PROFILES
learn their methods, see their studio spaces. Discover what inspires their work

HOW TO IMPROVE YOUR STUDIO
an efficiently laid out, clean woodworking studio is conducive to good work

DISCOVER HAND TOOL TECHNIQUES
grasp new methods of work. Increase your woodworking efficiency

DISCOVER TOOLS TO WORK WOOD
the why and how of tools to create joinery and smooth surfaces of wood

TABLE OF CONTENTS

FROM THE EDITOR 03
NORMAN PIROLLO

FURNITURE MAKER 04
LIVING THE DREAM

FURNITURE MAKER 14
THE JOURNEY

FURNITURE MAKER 24
SETTING UP SHOP

CRAIG THIBODEAU 30
MASTERY IN WOOD

GALLERY 38
FURNITURE & OBJECTS

THE MOXON VISE 46
RAISE YOUR WORK
TO NEW HEIGHTS

MAKING THE CASE 64
FOR LAMINATION

SIX STRATEGIES 76
TO IMPROVE YOUR
SHARPENING AND
WOODWORKING

DARRELL PEART 84
GREENE & GREENE

SOCIAL MEDIA 92
SPREAD THE WORD

WOOD FIGURE 102
HOW TO READ

CLOSING THOUGHTS 110

WOODSKILLS Magazine
Issue 02
2018/19

Editor
Norman Pirollo

Art Director
Linda Chenard

Layout
John Pirollo
Jonathan Cardone

Copy Editor
Norman Pirollo
Editorial Staff
Volunteers

Publisher
New Art Press

Contributors

Brian Greene
Darrell Peart
Jan Lennon
Craig Thibodeau
Norman Pirollo

Editorial Contributions
norman@woodskills.com

www.woodskills.com
twitter.com/WoodSkills
facebook.com/WoodSkills
Instagram: @woodskillsmag

FROM THE EDITOR

Welcome to Issue 02 of WOODSKILLS magazine. After careful analysis and research of existing woodworking magazines, our goal is create and deliver a unique, different type of publication. The magazine will only include a small selection of quality, curated advertising. WOODSKILLS magazine will primarily include fine woodworking articles and profiles of established woodworkers and furniture makers. These are woodworkers who excel at what they do and offer an insight into the techniques and work methods they have developed.

Included with each profile is the inspiration and philosophy behind the woodworker and furniture maker. Although machines are often used in the preliminary processing of wood, the vast majority of work in each WOODSKILLS article will be performed using a selection of quality hand tools. We sincerely hope you enjoy the magazine and look forward to producing quality content for your continued woodworking enjoyment.

Norman Pirollo

LIVING THE DREAM

An insight into the aspirations and defining moments in the quest to be a furniture maker. Critical discussion and realistic expectations.

by Norman Pirollo

If you are reading this article, chances are you dream of becoming a full-time furniture maker or at least a part-time furniture maker. The journey can be quick or instead more of a winding road. My journey to full-time furniture making was long with several challenges along the way. The primary hurdle was a financial one. A question that often crops up is how to survive while establishing yourself as a furniture maker. Today, it is not unusual to see woodworkers taking the leap into full-time furniture making within a few years. My hat goes off to these folks as they are more courageous than I ever was. In my case, the road to furniture making was gradual and included a stint in a part-time woodworking business.

Supporting myself was a primary consideration in the journey. Forsaking full-time employment was not an option unless my business income offset employment income. Adding to this, I was unsure whether being a full-time furniture maker would be the perfect creative outlet. So part-time woodworking it was, for at least several years. Assuming you have developed a passion for woodworking and often give thought to becoming a furniture maker. Do you dream of surviving off your woodworking passion? Maybe you are in a rut with your existing career, not deriving much satisfaction from a current job, or simply out of work. There are many reasons people dream about working at something they genuinely enjoy.

Workshop, hand tools and workbench all come together to create an environment conducive to woodworking. A peaceful, serene area in which we can unleash our creativity and develop hand to eye skills.

The thought of spending hours designing and creating tangible products can be a great source of satisfaction. In recent years, a growing cohort of people have embraced creativity in their lives. Furniture making as a living is appealing. Doing this for a living, either part-time or full-time, can be very rewarding and gratifying. So, you have taken the leap into being a furniture maker. The next logical step after becoming a furniture maker is to establish yourself as a business. Having started and developed four woodworking businesses, I can attest to the excitement of seeing a business grow. I like to tell people that if the business revolves around something you enjoy doing, success is assured. The title of this article refers to Living the Dream. The caveat to this statement is you need to be prepared of certain eventualities when creating furniture for others. Self-employment as a furniture maker provides independence. It creates a unique situation where you create furniture at your own pace, with no one looking over your shoulder. You are your own boss!

This article outlines and explains several other aspects of being a furniture maker. On the positive side, unlike many other fields, woodworking has been stable in its centuries-old evolution. The assumption here is that you embrace hand tools along with machinery in your furniture making. The use of hand tools is mentioned since the other extreme is a large movement towards the automation of furniture making. This article does not touch on automation, instead the focus here is traditional woodworking using basic tools and machinery. Many tools and machinery are in use today that date back a century or more. This gives you an idea of how relevant the knowledge you gain will continue to be useful and not become obsolete. In my business, I continue to use machinery and tools purchased over twenty years ago. The techniques used in my furniture making are the same as were taught to me thirty years ago.

MAKER EVOLUTION

Workshop, hand tools and workbench all come together to create an environment conducive to woodworking. A peaceful, serene area in which we can unleash our creativity and develop hand to eye skills.

Compared to the hi-tech industry, my knowledge and skills would be obsolete by today's standards. Creating tangible objects such as furniture provides a true sense of satisfaction and enjoyment. You can measure your productivity through the work you create. Working as a furniture maker will motivate you to perfect skills and techniques to create higher quality work. Businesses are inherently competitive. You will develop processes and improve on current ones to increase yield and improve your competitiveness. Over time, you will develop a better appreciation of your furniture making business. It can be overwhelming to grasp the many facets of being a full-time furniture maker. A primary concern will be to seek orders and commissions for your work. You need to evaluate the pros and cons of being a self-employed woodworker compared to holding a job.

A day job often provides stability and a regular source of income without worrying about the next pay check. We recognize this isn't always true, especially in today's rapidly evolving economy where the risk of downsizing or job loss is real. Until this occurs, a day job is a reliable source of income. If little to no satisfaction is gained from your work, consider becoming a part-time or full-time furniture maker. In my former career, I experienced downsizing and loss of employment on more than one occasion. This provided the motivation to develop a career I could rely on and become self-sufficient. The allure of furniture making held great appeal coming from a hi-tech background. Furniture making can be achieved with next to no technology and the need for constant updating is eliminated.

Workshop, hand tools and workbench all come together to create an environment conducive to woodworking. A peaceful, serene area in which we can unleash our creativity and develop hand to eye skills.

However, being in business for yourself involves much more than furniture making. There are other business aspects to consider. Other concerns include: accounting, inventory control, equipment and tool maintenance, purchasing, marketing, shipping, advertising and social media. You also need a substantial enough space to perform furniture making. It is crucial to factor all this into the time and cost of doing business. These aspects of business take valuable time away from the core furniture making but are fundamental for your business to survive and grow.

Today, there is an abundance of low-priced software to help manage a business and assist with accounting and bookkeeping. Software enables you to plug in numbers where the software performs all the background calculations for you. Over time, you will learn to manage these business-related tasks and revert to furniture making as your primary focus. I have not touched on the immense satisfaction derived from the independence of being a self-employed furniture maker. Speaking from personal experience, I can attest that the freedom gained is exceptional. You will no longer need to dress up and commute to a workplace that provides little satisfaction but only financial security.

Guaranteed jobs have also become a relic of the past. The often reduced and irregular income that comes with being a self-employed furniture maker is well worth it. A first step is to determine if you can survive as a furniture maker at this stage in your life. This is accomplished by weighing your fixed monthly costs which include housing, family expenses, vehicle expenses, food, utilities, etc. If you are the sole income earner, it might be challenging and stressful to survive monthly if business income is irregular and does not match your fixed monthly expenses. In this case, drawing a regular employment salary while building your new business is a more prudent approach.

EXPOSURE EDUCATION

Workshop, hand tools and workbench all come together to create an environment conducive to woodworking. A peaceful, serene area in which we can unleash our creativity and develop hand to eye skills.

Once you determine that your part-time business has grown to where you can survive from the income generated, give further thought to leaving your salaried job. People opt out of careers at some point in their lives to pursue their passion. I have done this and not regretted it. As a former hi-tech employee, I derive considerably more satisfaction today in my furniture making business. Self-employment is very rewarding!

In the decision to go into business, you need to evaluate the financial impact of generating your own income vs. deriving employment income. This applies to being self-employed regardless of the business. Furniture making is rewarding since you are pursuing your passion of creating tangible products where output is measured in real, physical terms. A key quality of success when striking out on your own is to have confidence in yourself.

A high level of confidence will spur you on where skepticism is your enemy. It is necessary to minimize the fear and insecurity of starting your own furniture making business. Self-confidence provides you the energy to offset any setbacks in the startup phase. Initially, mistakes in starting up a furniture making business are made or should I say, errors are made that are interpreted as mistakes. These are not mistakes and can be instead chalked up to naivety and lack of experience.

I recommend following a small business course before beginning. Options include a workshop on starting a business or mentoring with existing business owners and drawing on their expertise. The business owners do not need to be woodworkers, but it would speed the process up if they are. Community colleges offer small business courses and several business courses are available online today.

Workshop, hand tools and workbench all come together to create an environment conducive to woodworking. A peaceful, serene area in which we can unleash our creativity and develop hand to eye skills.

If you do not possess the required skills and expertise to be a furniture maker, study woodworking through a community college or woodworking school. Alternatively, apprentice with a knowledgeable woodworker, either as their assistant or in a mentor and student relationship. Many furniture makers are self-taught and progress from basic to advanced woodworking skills by creating piece after piece and studying existing woodworking principles. The process of teaching yourself these skills and techniques can be lengthy. If self-taught, no one can correct your mistakes or provide you guidance, although this approach is possible.

Early in my woodworking career, I struggled with some techniques, then followed a cabinetmaking program and returned to continue my woodworking. This progression resulted in better quality products and a much better understanding of woodworking. A few years later, I attended a fine furniture making school, the equivalent of following a master's program in woodworking. Classes were intense and woodworking occupied the whole day.

My woodworking skills dramatically increased after completing a series of classes. The takeaway is that you should not be averse to a formal education in woodworking. A large part of being a furniture maker involves marketing yourself. Exposure is critical to becoming a successful furniture maker. Advertising your business begins locally by handing out business cards at every opportunity. In the name of exposure, investigate opportunities where high-end crafts and furniture are exhibited.

Submit your best furniture pieces in an exhibition call for entry. Exposure gained from exhibitions and media is priceless to a furniture maker. Receiving awards at craft and furniture exhibitions validates you as an accomplished furniture maker. Media exposure is invaluable to getting the word out that you are a capable and skilled furniture maker. Following an exhibition, there is often an exhibition article written describing the entries and those that stand out are covered in depth.

MAKER SKILLS

Workshop, hand tools and workbench all come together to create an environment conducive to woodworking. A peaceful, serene area in which we can unleash our creativity and develop hand to eye skills.

As a furniture maker, it is also important to distinguish yourself as a furniture designer. The furniture designs you strive towards need to be more compelling than what is commonly available in the furniture market. To differentiate yourself from other furniture makers or commercial furniture, secondary or alternative mediums can be combined in your designs. Wood and metal are successful combinations.

Other elements include inlay, curved work, contrasting woods or intricate, visible joinery. You can also elect to make pieces in a furniture style popular in your area or region. This emphasis will draw a local clientele in. To accelerate your furniture design process, begin with sketches and drawings and progress to creating maquettes. Maquettes are small-scale models of furniture. The small-scale is so the maquette can be rapidly assembled using scraps of wood.

Since the maquette is a small-scale model, deficiencies in construction, stability or technical issues can be visualized though a three-dimensional view. Maquettes are a powerful tool in the design process. Working with CAD software is another tool available to today's furniture designer. Instead of drawing by hand and then creating a mockup or maquette; furniture designs could instead be drawn on a computer and then rendered.

The rendering process yields a 3-D view of the furniture. A 3-D view can be rotated. It is then straightforward to determine if the proportions and design are aesthetically pleasing. The CAD process accelerates the design process as well as providing software tools to create furniture plans. The 3-D views can then be shown to your clients for approval. Having said this, a scale mockup or maquette lends itself well to discovering structural issues in a design.

Workshop, hand tools and workbench all come together to create an environment conducive to woodworking. A peaceful, serene area in which we can unleash our creativity and develop hand to eye skills.

To recap, the dream is attainable and worth pursuing! When I eventually walked away from my former hi-tech career, it was a sense of relief. I could finally pursue my dream of being a full-time furniture maker and revel in the freedom of waking up to a new, fulfilling life. However, there will be struggles and challenges along the way. Unlike regular employment, there is no paycheck at the end of a weekly or two-week period. The onus is on you to acquire commissions. Marketing is key to your survival as a furniture maker. There is a distinct advantage to being a furniture maker today compared to only twenty years ago. The advantage is the Internet and social media.

Social media empowers us to successfully market ourselves at little cost. In my business, I use social media platforms such as Instagram, Facebook, Linkedin, YouTube and Twitter to my advantage. My clientele is no longer restricted to my immediate area or region. Social media allows a furniture maker to market themselves and their work on a national and international scale. Social media allows a furniture maker to develop a following or tribe with further access to each member's tribe.

This exponential effect results in exposure to tens of thousands of people. As a caveat, remaining relevant is critical through regular posting to social media platforms. I often create short videos and images of techniques or of workpieces currently on my workbench. People enjoy seeing what a maker is working on and follow you if they like your work and if you consistently post. A website is vital in marketing yourself as a furniture maker. A website provides information about yourself, your furniture making philosophy, and features an online gallery or portfolio of your work.

Clients today expect a furniture maker to have a regularly updated website. Large hosting companies make it simple to set up a website and populate it with information and images. Unlike a few years ago, the need to develop a website from scratch is eliminated. Be prepared, marketing and social media exposure will take time away from your studio work. You will eventually learn to manage time and set aside a few hours a week for marketing and social media.

Workshop, hand tools and workbench all come together to create an environment conducive to woodworking. A peaceful, serene area in which we can unleash our creativity and develop hand to eye skills.

Scale model or maquette of a wall-mounted wood art installation
Advertising and marketing promotional items, Pirollo Design

Workshop, hand tools and workbench all come together to create an environment conducive to woodworking. A peaceful, serene area in which we can unleash our creativity and develop hand to eye skills.

Newly designed hall table with wood and metal, 2009
Dovetailed set of drawers, 2008

Workshop, hand tools and workbench all come together to create an environment conducive to woodworking. A peaceful, serene area in which we can unleash our creativity and develop hand to eye skills.

FURNITURE MAKER JOURNEY

An insight into the aspirations and defining moments in the quest to be a furniture maker. This article chronicles a personal account of the journey.

by Norman Pirollo

The following narrative describe key parts of my journey of becoming a furniture designer + maker. Hopefully, this provides clarity of the struggle and overcoming negative aspects in your own journey. The positives outweigh negatives by far. Through this article, I hope to instill that it was in fact a journey to becoming a furniture maker. Although it may appear discouraging, coping with the difficulties strengthened me and confirmed my will to arrive at the destination. My goal was to seek validation as a furniture maker and be in a place where creating furniture would be second nature.

The period from 2005 through 2007 breathed new life into my woodworking. Although continuing to make and sell jewelry boxes, my focus shifted to larger pieces of furniture. As a follower and admirer of James Krenov, I became drawn to standalone cabinets since this was his signature style of furniture. Standalone cabinets were also portable and easily disassembled for transport. Figured woods could be selected for components of the cabinet.

The challenge of creating beautiful cabinets in the Scandinavian-inspired style of James Krenov, my new woodworking idol, would be rewarding. By late 2007, a series of courses were completed at the Rosewood Studio furniture making school. Afterwards, I was keen on building a first display cabinet featuring my newly acquired skills. Unlike the smaller jewelry boxes, there is a considerable investment in wood in a standalone cabinet. Although a cabinet built on spec (speculation) could be created with the intent to sell it, a commission is preferred.

In the next while I sought clients interested in owning such a cabinet. Not long after, I met with a friend and explained my situation. We discussed several options with mention she always wanted a large jewelry cabinet. Instead of a series of smaller jewelry boxes, she preferred a larger cabinet. A display cabinet configured as a jewelry armoire was immediately envisioned. The armoire would need to be large to accommodate her jewelry.

FURNITURE MAKER
THE JOURNEY

An insight into the aspirations and defining moments in the quest to be a furniture maker. This article chronicles a personal account of the journey

The cabinet could be outfitted with many drawers and dividers to hold her jewelry. More discussion ensued and with her approval, a few preliminary sketches of a design were drafted and rendered into larger scale drawings. After a follow-on meeting we agreed on the basic criteria of the design and price of the cabinet. The client gave me carte blanche and artistic license to include interesting elements to the design. We agreed on an Art Deco theme. Jewelry specific hardware such as revolving brass carousels for necklaces would be installed. Individual drawers would be lined with velvet and have dividers installed. The doors were frame and panel construction with curly maple panels.

Door and drawer pulls were carved from complementary woods. Blackwood and holly would be used together for a monochrome effect. The drawer fronts would be dovetailed into the sides. To hold true to James Krenov style, knife hinges would also be installed to hang the doors to the case. Having already built one cabinet using knife hinges, I felt comfortable with this choice. The cabinet sides, top, bottom, door rails and stiles would be Black Cherry. Cherry naturally ages over time and contrasts well with the lighter curly maple door panels. The cabinet stand would also be made from cherry. Since the design called for an Art Deco aesthetic, it was suggested to inlay diamond elements into the front of the cabinet.

Construction began on the jewelry armoire using methods of work recently gained through courses at Rosewood Studio. Hand tools formed a large percentage of the build. Hand planes and scrapers were used on the surfaces of the wood components. Prior to my education in fine furniture making, machines were used for a majority of the work with hand planes used for fitting. It was surprising at how much enjoyment I derived from the hand tool process. Dovetail joinery of drawer fronts was performed by hand using a previously designed dovetail jig. With a total of eight drawers, I hunkered down and created the dovetail joinery at one sitting.

(L) Installing bake-ins prior to veneering door panels.
(R) Knife hinge fitting

KRENOV DERIVED CASE CONSTRUCTION

Use of dowel joinery to attach sides to top and bottom panels

The case construction incorporated dowel joinery as per James Krenov process and style. Dowel joinery allowed top and bottom dimensions slightly larger than the depth and width of the case itself. The wide, deep top and bottom panels could have an edge profile applied and a chamfered edge was decided on. Improvements in the aesthetic of the cabinet could already be seen through the selection of wood. The components of the cabinet were both rift-sawn and quarter sawn. Proper grain matching resulted in harmony of wood graphics. The cabinet had a calm appearance without a clash of grain. If the wood components had been assembled without consideration to grain orientation, the cabinet would look odd and unnatural. The jewelry armoire was a success!

Over the next year, a shooting board was built to trim the end of small boards and components. More hand planes were also acquired, both new and used. Each of the hand planes provided a different functionality. A shoulder plane, a large metal-bodied jointer, and a few single use planes were purchased. With standard angle and low angle block planes, the standard angle block plane doubles as a small single-handed smoother.

I continued at my day job during this period. The struggle of juggling full-time employment with a part-time business was real. In my mind, I focused on the trajectory and destination. This effort would eventually lead to becoming a full-time furniture maker. Hopefully, the long days and weekends would ultimately pay off. The surfaces of furniture pieces were handplaned and scraped instead of sanded. While studying at Rosewood Studio, it was instilled in the students to not use sandpaper. Some sanding was allowed between finish coats when applying a finish, but wood surfaces were to be hand planed and scraped.

FURNITURE MAKER
THE JOURNEY

by Norman Pirollo

An insight into the aspirations and defining moments in the quest to be a furniture maker. This article chronicles a personal account of the journey

(L) Hand-cut dovetails, sawing tails.
(R) Bevel-edge chisels to work on drawer components

The de-emphasis of sanding was also the case at College of the Redwoods, where James Krenov taught. It was believed handplaned and scraped wood surfaces imparted a greater depth and clarity while sanded surfaces were dull. Scraping and planing would cleanly slice wood fibers where sanding abraded and made them fuzzy. I firmly believed in this approach after seeing and experiencing it myself.

There was a side effect to the newly gained hand tool philosophy of work. Improvements were made to my jewelry box process through use of a shooting board to trim small components. Accurately cut pieces resulted from applying this method. The surfaces of the jewelry boxes were then scraped and handplaned while in the past machines and sanding would suffice. These enhancements raised the quality of the jewelry boxes to a new level. With the final days of 2007 approaching, thought was given to a new direction. Although continuing to produce jewelry boxes, I felt a larger calling.

The creation of larger scale furniture pieces would satisfy a desire in me to achieve a loftier goal in woodworking. In late 2007, the new focus of standalone cabinets excited me. By following this path, similar work to that of James Krenov became achievable. At the time, I believed in no better cabinet designs. After all, James Krenov launched the Scandinavian inspired furniture movement.

With a new emphasis on creating furniture, I decided on a clean break from White Mountain Design. I would instead form a new dedicated furniture making business. Until this time, furniture, jewelry boxes, humidors and hand planes were combined into my existing website with categories for each. This might confuse a client seeking to acquire my work. After exhaustive research and several name combinations, the name Refined Edge Design was selected.

KRENOV DERIVED CASE CONSTRUCTION

Doweling jig to accurately drill holes

The name had appeal as it spoke to the refined edges of my furniture. After tossing the name around to a few individuals, the consensus was it accurately described my workmanship as well as being on point. The next steps involved registering the business name, setting up a new website and populating it with recently completed furniture pieces. The added expense of hosting another website was worthwhile in my opinion. A new logo would also need to be designed along with new business cards and marketing material. Development of the Refined Edge Design business was completed early in 2008. The business motivated me to place a greater emphasis on furniture making. Initial feedback showed my new series of standalone cabinets had great appeal.

The attention to detail, dovetail joinery, inlay and other elements fascinated people as these features were not available in mass-produced furniture. Two additional standalone cabinets were designed and built within the year, each one created from different woods. Popular woods included cherry, beech and maple. Each of these woods have unique characteristics and different densities. Maple is slightly harder and denser than cherry, beech has a density between that of cherry and maple. Edge profiles are more durable and workable on denser woods. However, all three woods exhibit optimal characteristics for furniture construction.

Late in 2007, the last of a series of courses had been completed at Rosewood Studio. The last courses focused on detail work, inlay and small projects. A prominent American woodworker, Garrett Hack, taught several of the courses. One course had a demi-lune table as the project. Each student had to complete a table during the course, or come close to completion. The demi-lune table is unique in that the front apron rail is curved. It wraps around the front and sides of the table to create a crescent-shaped tabletop.

FURNITURE MAKER
THE JOURNEY

by Norman Pirollo

An insight into the aspirations and defining moments in the quest to be a furniture maker. This article chronicles a personal account of the journey

In this class, we had to create the angled tenons that attach the curved rail to the back legs by hand. This interesting exercise involved several calculations. A second course with Garrett Hack involved the design and build of a wall-mounted cabinet. The cabinet was constructed of clear pine with a lapped cedar back and a raised cherry door panel. The cabinet had a single door. The components of the small cabinet were created and shaped using hand tools. Each student had some artistic license to add additional elements to the design. This course provided me with knowledge of creating wall cabinets.

During this period, I discovered the developing phenomenon of blogging. Blogging was in its infancy but rapidly becoming popular. Thought was given to writing blog posts about furniture created in my workshop. Posts could also be written about my methods of work, furniture designs and woodworking philosophy. This became very appealing since I enjoyed writing.

An initial blog was created in early fall 2007 and entries were posted, typically every three days. Each post would also include an image or two. The blog, The Refined Edge, grew in popularity and a considerable following developed. I enjoy blogging and continue to blog about woodworking today. With a new emphasis on cabinets, the need turned to developing new marketing channels. Shipping cabinets of this size could get complicated and costly.

The preference became to establish a local market for my work. My city is large although not as large as nearby urban centers. Since the large urban centers of Toronto and Montreal were a only few hours away, transporting furniture on my own to these centers was a viable option. The real challenge would be to educate people on the benefits of one of a kind, heirloom furniture and the customization options available.

Dovetailed drawers with alternate dovetail layout ratios shown

KRENOV DERIVED CASE CONSTRUCTION

Use of rabbet and lip technique to conceal door overlay

Several thoughts and ideas raced through my mind. With jewelry boxes, a few could easily be created on spec and eventually sold. The more popular models of jewelry boxes were created in small batches. With larger cabinets, this approach was no longer feasible. Since there would be a unique design and customization with each cabinet, it could not be solely produced on (spec) speculation. It became necessary to acquire a commission from a client along with a down payment for materials. This describes the standard method of doing commission work. A formal contract would also need to be signed between the client and myself. The contract included completion dates and an accurate estimate of the cost of the cabinet. Both standalone cabinets and wall-mounted cabinets were offered. By 2008, my financial situation improved to where my furniture making studio could be equipped with a few more wall-mounted tool cabinets, a dedicated plane rack and more hand planes. The wall mounted plane rack design was modeled after existing designs. The hand planes sit in angled compartments, making it easy to grab the correct hand plane for a task.

Over the course of the year, a new piece of machinery came into my possession. I was informed of an opportunity to purchase a vintage wide bed jointer. Until this time, the only jointer in my shop had a narrow 6-inch bed. This limited the width of boards to be jointed and prepared. The vintage jointer had a 9.25-inch wide bed with longer input and output beds. This allowed me to maintain the width of most rough boards and was a boon to my workflow. In mid-2008, another of the standalone cabinets was being designed and built. This cabinet had a cleaner design and featured fully veneered front doors. I wanted to feature unique grain graphics on the doors. Assembling doors using frame and panel construction considerably reduced the size of the panel graphics. Fully veneered doors allowed more door area to display exciting figure. A fully veneered method of door construction would also provide me with an exciting challenge.

The sides and back were of conventional solid wood construction. The back was assembled using frame and panel construction to stay true to the James Krenov philosophy of furniture making. He believed the back of a furniture piece should be well made and as beautiful as the front. Typically, in modern furniture, the back of furniture is inexpensively put together since it is assumed the furniture will be against a wall. Installing a frame and panel back would allow it to be seen when the front doors are opened, adding to the interior beauty of a cabinet. Although this step involved considerably more work, the results were well worth it.

I designed and built the upper cabinet and then created the stand for the cabinet. Creating the cabinet and stand as individual units allowed me to make the stand more accurate in dimensions. The cabinet would perfectly conform to the base of the cabinet. The upper cabinet and stand were also designed to be separated, for ease of transport and handling. This second cabinet featured fewer drawers in the interior than the earlier cabinet. Instead, I wanted to create more display space for valuable art objects such as vases and bowls. The added interior height allowed for three lower drawers, arranged in an asymmetric layout.

Another feature of the cabinet was the plain uniformity of the wood surfaces. A light color had been decided on and European Beech was used to accomplish this. European Beech does not have a pronounced grain pattern, instead it appears very plain and nondescript. This grain pattern or graphic became the intended effect for the cabinet exterior. The only dramatic part of the cabinet was the exciting, book-matched graphics integral to the front doors. Several months later, Lark Books featured the Twin Plumes cabinet in the forward of their 500 Cabinets book.

Marking & creating mortise for custom door pull

Creating mortise for custom drawer pull

KRENOV DERIVED CASE CONSTRUCTION

Fitted frame and panel cabinet back

This summarizes my transition to furniture making. It is only after being exposed to making furniture pieces that I realized this to be my true calling. The series of furniture making courses also increased confidence in my ability to pursue a career in furniture making. The earlier period of box making provided an exceptional learning curve of working with small casework.

As mentioned earlier, standalone and wall-mounted cabinets were viewed as scaled up boxes. The construction parameters were similar, larger dimensioned panels being the only real change. Creating and installing two mating front doors became a critical technique to master. Making conventionally scaled furniture pieces allowed me to experiment with techniques such as book-matched front doors. The larger expanse of wood in these cabinets would do justice to the graphics attained through veneering.

The Twin Plumes cabinet is an excellent example of incorporating book-matched, veneered doors into a cabinet design. This feature causes the cabinet to stand out with an art aesthetic. It is during this period of roughly four years (2005-2008) that I established myself as a furniture maker. The next step in the evolution was to break away from conventional square or rectangular casework and embrace a curved, organic aesthetic. This is not so much a departure but rather the addition of new techniques and processes to my existing skills!

FURNITURE MAKER
SETTING UP SHOP

by Norman Pirollo

Discussion of the essential tools and space requirements in setting up a furniture making space. Valuable insight from an established furniture maker.

TOOLS & MACHINES

Furniture is created using machinery and power tools, using only hand tools or a combination of both. Production-oriented furniture making shops use machines to maximize efficiency and speed production of furniture. Small furniture makers instead use a hybrid selection of machines and hand tools in their shops. Machines are used to prepare and process lumber to create furniture. Small power tools and hand tools are used to create the joinery in furniture.

Hand planes are used for final smoothing of wood surfaces. Hand tools are later used for detail work and finishing. As a small furniture maker, you should invest in some machinery. Machinery is used to process lumber for conversion from rough-sawn to processed boards. The boards are then dimensioned for use in furniture making. Typical machines include a jointer, planer, and a bandsaw or table saw.

Although processing and dimensioning of wood can be performed using hand saws, the labor involved can be overwhelming. A bandsaw is highly recommended as one of the most versatile machines in furniture making. With an emphasis today on minimizing dust in woodworking environments, efficient dust control is critical. All machines and small power tools generate dust, either fine airborne dust or larger particulates. The health of your lungs should be a priority in your work environment. Dust control is installed at the source and is the preferred method of capturing dust before it becomes airborne. Dust control takes the form of central dust collectors or cyclonic dust collectors. Piping or tubing begins at the source or machine and leads back to a central dust collector. An air cleaner should also be installed in your shop to remove airborne dust. Airborne dust is what you breathe. Since this fine dust is light, it will float for a considerable time in a shop environment. The air cleaner cycles shop air through it and within minutes will scrub a shop environment of fine airborne dust.

Recommended equipment for a furniture making shop:

Jointer (6 in. to 8 in. wide)
Planer (13 in. to 15 in. wide)
Bandsaw (14 in. to 17 in. throat)
Tablesaw (2HP or 3HP model)
Drill Press (16 in. floor-mounted)
Router Table (2HP to 3HP plunge type)
Horizontal Mortiser (to create mortises)

This list reflects machinery installed in a typical furniture making shop. Another facet in furniture making involves hand tools, used exclusively or in conjunction with machines. Hand tools provide greater control of a woodworking process. Machines excel when efficiency and repeatability are sought. Hand tools provide a tactile element to the process.

Over the years, my style of work has evolved where today I embrace the use of hand tools in my furniture making. I have devised methods of work to increase efficiency when using hand tools. Hand tools have their place in most furniture making shops today.

Hand tools to consider for furniture making:

Set of Chisels (to create mortises and dovetails)
Hand Planes (preparing and finishing surfaces)
Squares (for precision and accuracy)
Workbench (with a front and tail vise)
Dovetail saw (to create dovetail joinery)
Rip saw (for ripping wood)
Back saw (for crosscutting)
Shooting Board (for precise end cuts)
Bench Hook (for accurate trimming)

Using hand tools initially results in a much slower process than using machines. Over time, you will find that the efficiency gained from using hand tools offsets the productivity gains of machines. Machines need regular maintenance and setup that needs to be factored into the overall time necessary to build furniture. I favor a hybrid shop environment where machines and hand tools are used together. Over time, you will develop an effective workflow and likely re-arrange workbenches and machines in your shop. Through an improved workflow, your productivity will increase.

There are instances where woodworkers work only with hand tools. Often, the reason is that they have developed a woodworking philosophy of working exclusively with hand tools. Another reason is they cannot run noisy or dusty machinery at their locations. A third reason is they prefer the hand tool process and the accompanying peacefulness and quiet that comes with it. For example, you can live in a condominium setting and create furniture in a spare room. It is entirely possible to accomplish this using only hand tools and a solid, proper woodworking bench. The hand tool approach minimizes noise and dust and you can work any time of the day or evening without disturbing family or neighbors. If you decide on hand tools as a component of your furniture making, it will be necessary to become familiar with sharpening processes.

FURNITURE MAKER
SETTING UP SHOP

Discussion of the essential tools and space requirements in setting up a furniture making space. Valuable insight from an established furniture maker.

Hand tools require regular sharpening to be effective. A blunt chisel is a dangerous tool since the greater force necessary to slice through wood can lead to injury. I always maintain my hand tools, especially chisel and hand plane blades, to a high degree of sharpness. You will find that sharp hand tools will make your furniture making safer and more enjoyable. Over time, you will develop best practices in your furniture making. Best practices instill efficiency and quality in furniture making. Jigs can be developed to create repeatability of furniture components. If creating a large series of similar chairs, jigs will speed the creation of chair components. The use of jigs also ensures each component will precisely fit multiple chairs. Jigs can be reused on a furniture series you plan on marketing for several years. Precision and repeatability are ensured through use of woodworking jigs. Some jigs are used for a unique operation where other jigs are more versatile. I use a fair number of jigs in my furniture making.

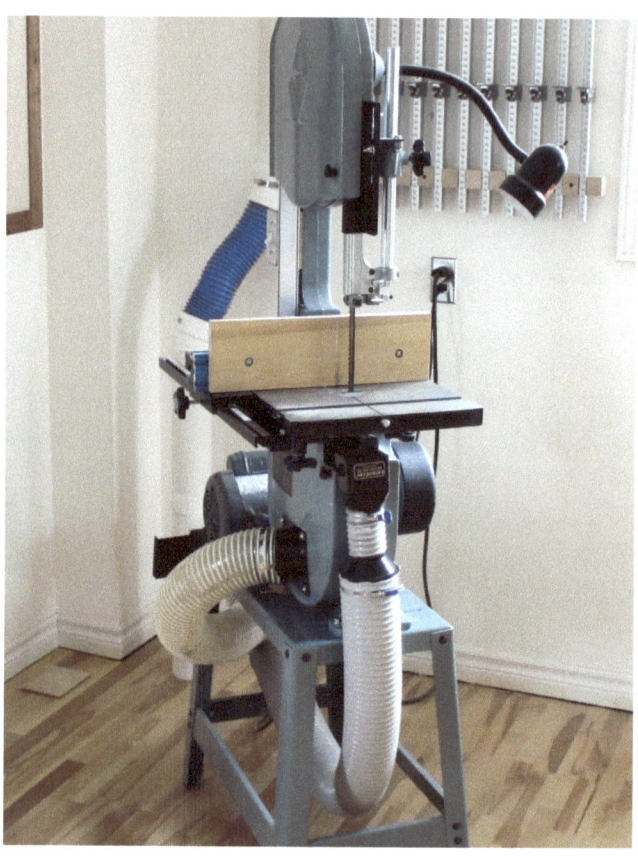

SPACE

Space requirements for a furniture making shop vary. Some furniture makers work on several furniture pieces at a time while others work on individual pieces. Other makers work primarily with hand tools and minimal use of machinery. If the space is small, it is best to work with hand tools and minimal use of machines. With an emphasis on hand tools, workshop space requirements are in the order of 200 square feet. If you build larger furniture or work in small batches, space requirements increase substantially. If your furniture making is machinery intensive, space requirements will increase to accommodate machines. A machinery-intensive shop environment will need a minimum of 600 square feet of space.

Each machine requires space around it for safe operation and maneuvering boards within its radius. In many furniture making environments, machine and bench areas are separate. The noise and dust associated with machines is then isolated from the bench area of the shop. Dust reduction can be accomplished by installing a swinging door or heavy, overlapping, vertically hung plastic strips. A best practice is to locate the bench room in its own enclosed room or space. Another component of a furniture making shop is the assembly area. This is where furniture is dry-fitted, assembled and later glued together. An area in the shop also needs to be reserved for applying finish to furniture. This finishing space needs to be relatively dust free.

Stickered lumber is stored in another area of the shop. Stickering allows each board to be separate from the other or laid vertically against a wall in bins. Lumber can either be laid flat or vertical. If vertical, the lumber is more accessible and individual boards can be more easily separated and pulled out. It is critical to let the wood breathe and acclimate to the furniture making area. Therefore, plenty of open space surrounding the wood is necessary. Other considerations in furniture making are higher than normal ceilings to swing longer planks around without hitting light fixtures. In my studio, nine-foot ceilings have been installed. It is also recommended to have copious amounts of ambient and artificial light in your shop.

THE FOCAL POINT OF A FURNITURE MAKING STUDIO IS THE VERSATILE WORKBENCH

Invest in a high-quality, rigid bench or custom build your own.

There are banks of dual fluorescent fixtures in my studio. The banks are switched separately depending on the amount of light necessary at any time of day or evening. An investment was made in several large windows to bring in as much ambient light as possible. The large windows cut down on the need for artificial light. When light is necessary for a bench operation or when using a machine, task lighting can be set up to provide additional lighting. Task lighting eliminates the need to turn on the main shop lights. The overhead shop lamps are connected in two separate banks in my furniture making studio. To summarize, a furniture making shop can operate in as small as 200 sq. ft. or ideally in 600 sq. ft. space and above. Depending on your workflow, if working on a single furniture piece at a time, a small space will suffice.

If you intend to work in multiples or small batches with several furniture pieces at a time, a larger space is necessary. Also critical in determining workshop size is the ratio of hand tool use to machinery in your furniture making. Machines demand more space while hand tools are limited to a workbench or two. To make the most effective use of a space, my furniture studio comprises two levels one above the other. This allows me to maintain a defined square footage and instead build vertically. This is something to consider in the design of your own furniture making studio. In recent years, I have also embraced a minimalistic view of things. It is preferable to leave open spaces than to fill every nook and cranny with a machine or bench and create clutter in the process. An open and clutter-free environment lends itself well to a more efficient and productive workflow!

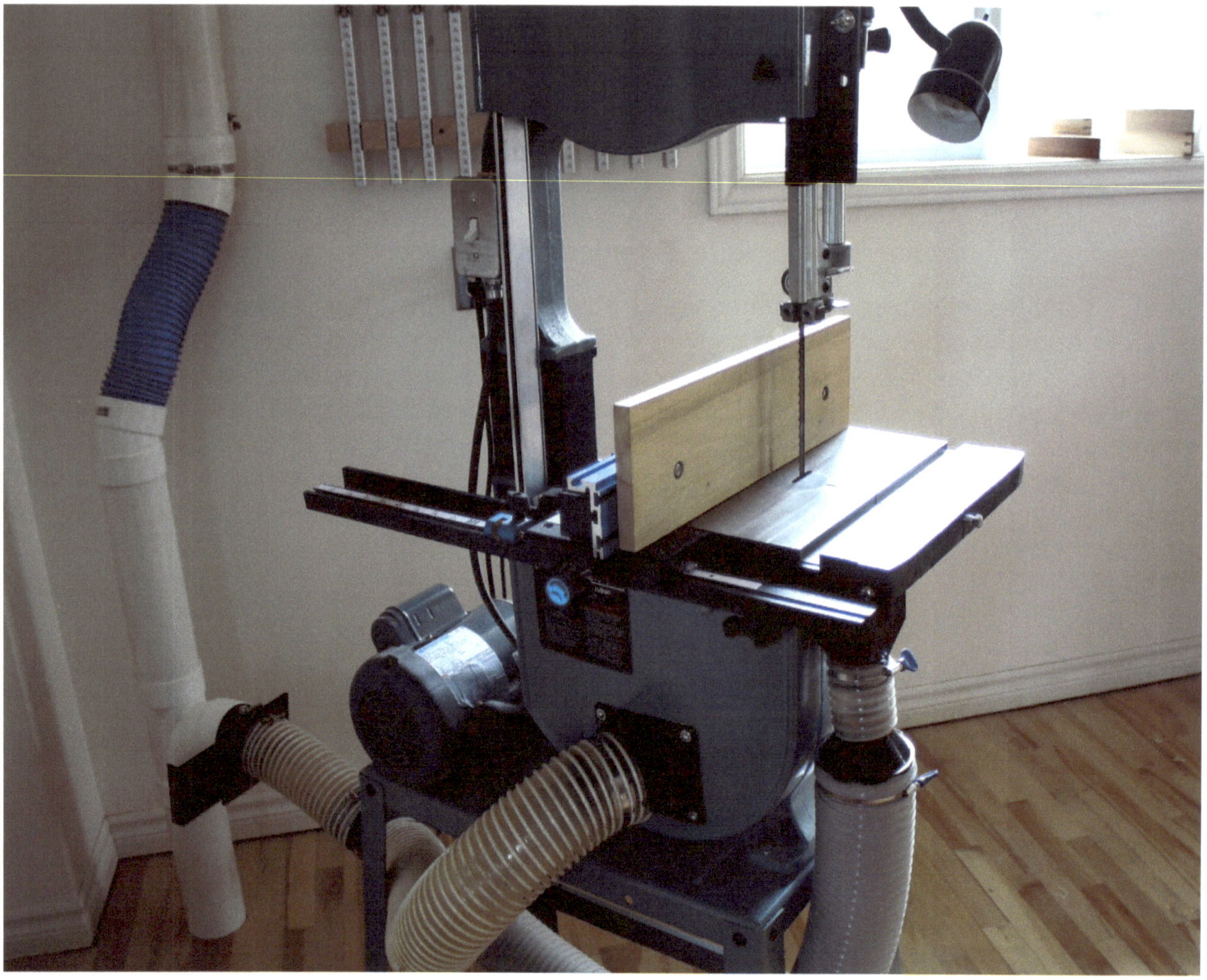

The versatile bandsaw is the mainstay of a workshop and can be substituted for a table saw
Machines, workbenches and hand tools are combined in a modern furniture making studio

Wall-mounted lumber rack has a low profile and convenient access
Sliding miter sled for a table saw provides accuracy, repeatability and safety

Photo by Craig Carlson

CRAIG THIBODEAU
MASTERY IN WOOD
by Norman Pirollo

A conversation with a woodworker and furniture maker who combines traditional marquetry with contemporary design in his furniture pieces. His fascinating journey and inspiration are discussed.

The very first thing noticed in Craig Thibodeau's work is the intricateness and attention to detail. Craig excels at incorporating marquetry and veneer work in his furniture designs. He has developed a unique aesthetic that combines tradition with contemporary design. The art of marquetry dates back to the 18th century, Craig has embraced it and follows in the tradition of early masters. He has studied with top contemporaries in his field and gleaned the centuries old craft of marquetry in the process. The unique characteristic of patience is critical to fine marquetry and Craig exudes this in spades. Often spending large amounts of time working on intricate detail, the slow, methodical approach works best for him. Complex inlay patterns, floral and animal motifs pop his furniture designs.

This detail is testament to the years of expertise behind Craig's work. Not content with the static beauty of his furniture pieces, Craig has been incorporating interactivity into furniture pieces. This is accomplished through complex mechanical and puzzle mechanisms. The common theme in all this is how Craig enjoys delving into and rediscovering age old traditions in furniture making. He then adds his own unique twist to these traditions. The prevalent genre of Craig's work is Art Deco, a style seen in several of his pieces. To summarize, Craig has taken furniture making to the next level through marquetry, inlay and mechanical movements. We look forward to seeing more of Craig's exciting work in the future and how his aspirations in furniture making unfold.

WS: How and when did you decide to become a woodworker?

CT: I don't think I made a conscious decision early on to become a woodworker but I always had a workshop of some kind either in a garage or storage unit, even while going to college I had a shop to work in on the weekends. Right about the time my first child was born I decided I'd rather be at home working and able to spend time with my kids than gone all day at a day job in an office..

WS: Growing up, who and what inspired you to follow a path in woodworking?

CT: Well, we always had a workshop in the garage growing up though I don't recall ever really using it to make anything. Both my parents worked in their shop doing a variety of jobs from woodworking to tool maintenance so I was exposed to a shop environment from early on even if I didn't realize the influence it would have on me later.

WS: You are a furniture designer, maker. What kinds of furniture do you design + make and in what styles?

CT: The short answer is that I design and make whatever style my current client wants. The majority of my work is custom commissions so I spend most of my design time creating pieces that suit the current clients needs and desires. When time allows I will make speculation work for galleries and shows and it is often in either an Art Deco or Asian/Arts and Crafts style. Typically, these pieces will showcase some new style of marquetry I've been wanting to explore. As these pieces gain exposure they tend to spawn additional work in a similar style.

WS: What attracted you to the Art Deco style of furniture?

CT: Probably the complexity, Art Deco furniture involves highly complex veneering and inlay and demands a tremendous amount of skill and patience from the maker. Some of the more elaborate Art Deco furniture designs from the 1920's might take hundreds of hours of labor to create and I find the challenge intriguing.

WS: What inspired you to begin incorporating marquetry and parquetry in your furniture designs? In a few words, can you describe both these techniques?

CT: Seeing the work of marquetry master Paul Schurch at a number of shows inspired me to contact him to take one of his classes in marquetry, luckily he was still teaching marquetry in his shop and I was able to take a week long class from him and learn the fundamentals of marquetry which really jump started my marquetry career. The parquetry work I do came from the need to fulfill a client commission, I taught myself how to do parquetry because of a large commission years ago that incorporated a variety of parquetry decoration.

WS: Your marquetry process involves the Boulle method. Were you self-taught in this traditional 18th century Boulle method? Did you attend formal training to learn this method? Can you enlighten us to the background of this method?

CT: Turns out I forgot to change this info on my website, I actually use the packet method which differs from the Boulle method. The packet method involves cutting all the various layers of the image at once and is a technique I learned from Paul Schurch when I took my first marquetry class from him in 2005.

OAK LEAF MARQUETRY (DETAIL) CURLY MAPLE, WENGE, VARIOUS MARQUETRY WOODS
Craig Thibodeau San Diego, CA USA

LILY BUFFET, 2007   WENGE, VAVONA, VARIOUS MARQUETRY WOODS
42" H x 32" W x 15" D Craig Thibodeau San Diego, CA USA

Photo by Craig Carlson

WS: What hand tools do you use most often when working with inlay and decorative elements in a furniture piece?

CT: It really depends on the specific job I'm doing, many of my hand tools are inlay specific whether small chisels I've made from jeweler's files or other more miniature size tools. Quite frequently my inlay work actually starts with a Dremel tool mounted in a special base and fitted with small solid carbide bits. Once the main material removal work is done I break out my miniature chisels and files to do the cleanup work. To cut the inlay materials themselves I actually usually use a scroll saw with a 2/0 blade, reconstituted stone and mother of pearl cut easily enough with slow speed and the right blades. Once the inlay pieces are cut jewelers files do a nice job of cleaning up the cut edges and reshaping profiles. Scalpels are another handy tool to have around as they can be used to scribe around the perimeter of an inlay or to clean up the sharp corners of a routed recess where the router can't reach.

WS: Have you have mastered marquetry, parquetry and inlay or do you feel you have more to learn?

CT: I'm not sure it's possible to master any of these techniques actually. I've seen work from several marquetry experts in the UK that is many times more complex than my work and would require much more time than I have to dedicate to the work. My marquetry work is what I would describe as a cartoonish representation of flowers; they aren't meant to look like real flowers or have the subtle complexity of real flowers. They just give the viewer the impression of bright floral arrangements and flowing floral vines. There are many marquetry makers that create designs far more complex and detailed than mine but I have decided on a particular look for my work that at the moment I am content with, perhaps in the future there will be time to learn new techniques with more complexity. The same can be said for parquetry and inlay, I am skilled at the specific work I choose to create but there are many more skills to learn in any of these specific fields. A lifetime could be spend attempting to perfect any of them and I am just at the tip of the iceberg.

WS: In a few of your pieces you incorporate mechanical movements and puzzle mechanisms? You obviously have a mechanical aptitude. What are the origins of featuring these complex mechanisms in your work? Is there a historical precedence of including mechanical elements in furniture?

CT: My background is as a mechanical engineer so I suppose I have always had an interest in mechanical mechanisms and moving parts. I began incorporating these mechanisms in my furniture a few years ago after seeing some the work by David Roentgen from the 17th and 18th century in a video from the Metropolitan Museum on YouTube. The pieces he created with a team of watchmakers, jewelers and furniture makers is mind blowing in complexity. It astounds me that he was able to create pieces of such complexity at a time when there were no computers, no CAD, no CNC and only minimal equipment.

Roentgen wasn't the only one making mechanical furniture in that time, there were a number of makers creating highly complex mechanical work around the same time period. There seems to have been a market for these one of a kind pieces with the extremely wealthy of that age that doesn't exist in the same form now. The mechanical movements I have in my work are just the very beginnings of what can be done mechanically in furniture and I hope to continue exploring more complex designs as time allows. This is a field I wish to delve into in much greater detail.

WS: How would you describe your current work and what inspires it?

CT: My current work continues to explore mechanical movement and I've begun incorporating puzzle mechanisms into the furniture as a way of making the furniture more interactive. I've become a bit bored with making more traditional furniture and want my work to have something more, at the moment the something more is mechanics and puzzles. One day it might just be something else but for the moment I'm enjoying creating pieces that are interactive and mechanically complex. I can't say what specifically inspires this type of work as there really aren't very many folks making pieces like these (you could count them on one hand and still have a few fingers left over) but I suppose it still goes back to the work of David Roentgen, seeing his furniture started me on the journey into mechanical furniture and I'm just seeing where that will take me.

Photo by Craig Carlson

SERPENTINE MEDIA CENTER, 2015   WENGE, SPRUCE   34" H x 102"W x 20" D
Craig Thibodeau San Diego, CA USA

Photo by Craig Carlson

PUZZLE CABINET, 2014 ETIMOE, AMBOYNA BURL, CURLY SYCAMORE, MAPLE BURL, EBONY, MARQUETRY WOODS 34" H x 42"W x 18" D Craig Thibodeau San Diego, CA USA

WS: Do you have a favorite piece? If so, which one and why?

CT: Not really, I have a few pieces I've made several times in different materials that I quite like, my Art Deco chess table is one of those pieces and I do have a fondness for that particular piece as it was one of the first truly original Art Deco pieces I designed. It seems to have garnered some appreciation with clients as I have made it in a number of versions in different materials over the years. Beyond that my favorite piece is usually the one I'm currently working on and as soon as it's complete I'm ready to move on to the next piece.

WS: Which woods do prefer working with and why?

CT: I really don't have any preference for specific woods, some are easy to work and some are difficult but whichever one looks best in the current project is the one I'll use. My current mechanical puzzle cabinet is made primarily of Walnut and it is a joy to work compared to the previous piece made in Wenge, which is a real pain to work sometimes.

WS: Are there any mediums and methods you have not yet explored but hope to in the future?

CT: I've been doing a bit more metal work over the past year and find it both interesting and exhausting compared to woodworking. I would like to incorporate more detailed metal work in certain pieces in the future but for the moment I outsource the fabrication of more complex parts to local machine shops. I would also like to do a bit more hand tool work in my woodworking as time allows. I won't be hand cutting dovetails anytime soon but I'd like to move in that direction, it would be nice to find a way to slow things down in the shop a bit and now feel the push to complete every piece on a tight deadline. Hand tool work seems like it would help facilitate that slowing down process.

WS: To date, what has been the most rewarding experience involving your furniture and being a furniture designer + maker?

CT: Probably the fact that I've somehow been able to make ends meet and keep our bills paid for 18 years with just my furniture work, hopefully that will continue well into the future.

WS: What advice would you give to someone who is aspiring to become a woodworker and furniture designer?

CT: That's a tough question. I have always partially regretted being self taught, I think things might have been easier had I gone to a furniture making school like College of the Redwoods or North Bennet Street. Then again, I might be doing something completely different had I done that. I would suggest that taking classes from someone skilled in the thing you want to learn is a great way to jump start your progress in any field. It's even more beneficial if you can take a class in that person's shop and get a feel for how they run a business. In the end it takes time and effort to get good at anything and you've got to be willing to work hard to get to the place you want to be, it won't happen overnight but it will eventually if you work hard and stay focused on whatever goal you decide to set for yourself.

WS: What are you currently working on that you would like to mention?

CT: I'm working on another puzzle/mechanical cabinet that spins 360 degrees and has a variety of different mechanical locks and puzzle mechanisms that open and close as the cabinet rotates. Hopefully one more in a long line of this type of piece.

Photo by Craig Carlson

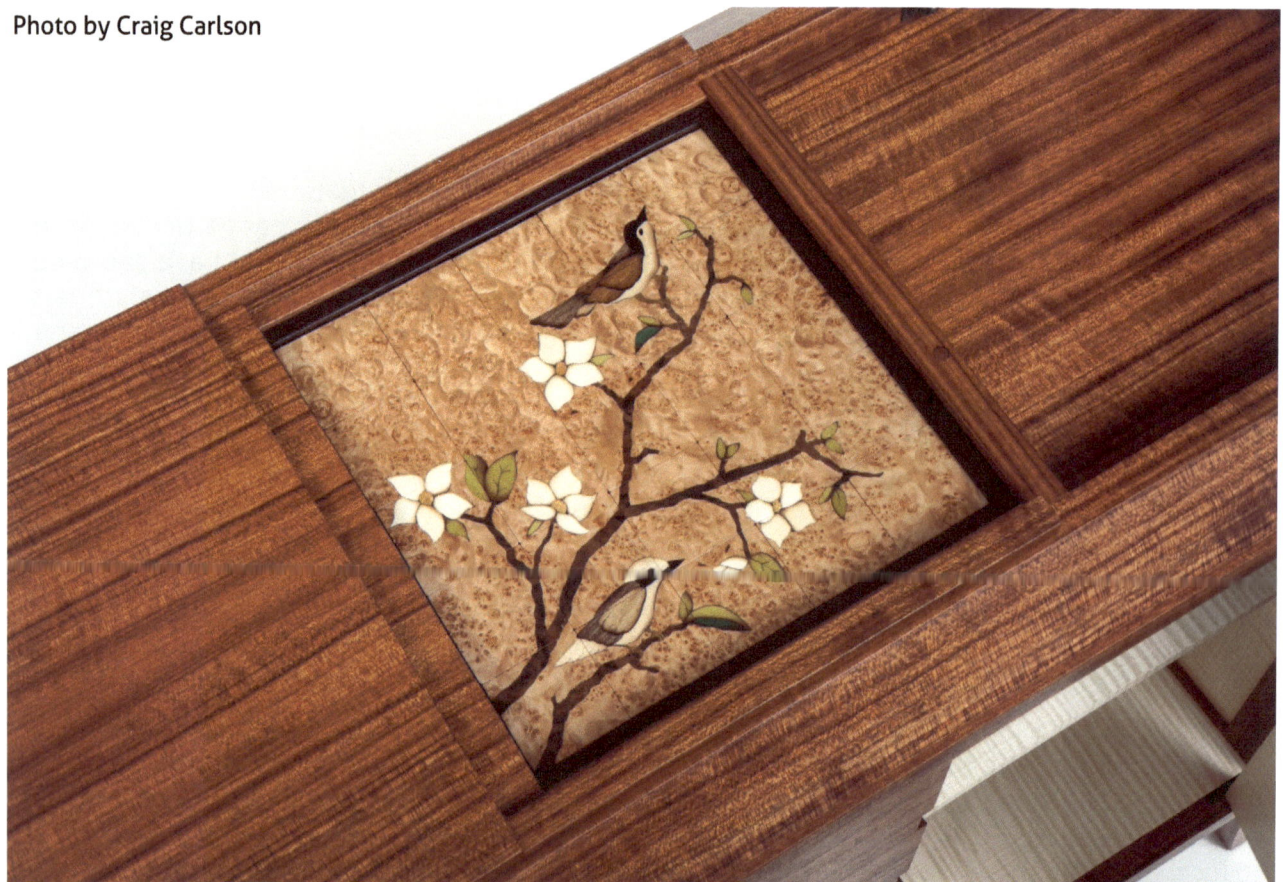

PUZZLE CABINET (Detail), 2014 ETIMOE, AMBOYNA BURL, CURLY SYCAMORE, MAPLE BURL, EBONY, MARQUETRY WOODS 34" H x 42"W x 18" D
Craig Thibodeau San Diego, CA USA

WS: Are there any upcoming projects, books and/or events that you would like to mention?

CT: Well I do have a book on veneering coming out on October 16, 2018 with the Taunton Press so I think that's certainly worth a mention. It is intended for anyone interested in veneering no matter the skill level; the text covers everything that a beginner would need to know to get started with veneer but also presents more advanced techniques for makers with some veneering skills; things like marquetry, parquetry, curved veneering, etc. I really poured everything I've learned over the years into the book in the hopes that it would help someone interested in learning and save them some of the troubles I experienced early on in my career.

Photo by Craig Carlson

WISTERIA CABINET, 2017 HONDURAN MAHOGANY,, MAPLE BURL, AMBROYNA BURL, WALNUT BURL, WALNUT, SYCAMORE, OLIVE ASH, MARQUETRY WOODS 70" H x 36"W x 20" D
Craig Thibodeau San Diego, CA USA

GALLERY
CRAIG THIBODEAU

MAPLE LEAF CABINET, 2010
MAHOGANY, SPALTED MAPLE, EUCALYPTUS, MARQUETRY WOODS

34" H x 42" W x 16" D

Craig Thibodeau
San Diego, CA
USA

Photo by Craig Carlson

JAPANESE PARQUETRY BOX, 2017 DOUGLAS FIR, FUMED LARCH, SYNTHETIC OPAL, EBONY, GOLD MOTHER OF PEARL   4" H x 16" W x 9" D Craig Thibodeau San Diego, CA USA

Photo by Craig Carlson

DIAMOND CABINET, 2008
JATOBA, MAPLE, SAPELE

34" H x 42" W x 20" D

Craig Thibodeau
San Diego, CA
USA

Photo by
Craig Carlson

AUTOMATON TABLE (OPEN), 2015
PAU FERRO, QUILTED MAPLE, EBONY, BIRD'S EYE MAPLE, STAINLESS STEEL

34" H x 24" W x 24" D

Craig Thibodeau
San Diego, CA
USA

Photo by
Craig Carlson

GALLERY
DARRELL PEART

AURORA CHEST OF DRAWERS, 2003 MAHOGANY, EBONY
60" H x 37" W x 26" D Darrell Peart Seattle, WA USA
Photo by Richard McNamee

TALL CORNER TABLE, 2017 SAPELE, EBONY
35" H x 26" W x 17.5" D Darrell Peart Seattle, WA USA
Photo by Darrell Peart

GALLERY
JAN LENNON

MEALA DRESSING / CONSOLE TABLE,, 2017 BLACK WALNUT, OLIVE ASH, MDF, FLEXIPLY
798mm H x 470mm W x 1208mm L   Jan Lennon United Kingdom

EXMOOR ARMCHAIR,
2018
SOLID EUROPEAN OAK,
LOURO PRETO, WALNUT
DETAIL

760mm H x 720mm W
x 660mm L

Jan Lennon
United Kingdom

Photos by Jan Lennon

GALLERY READERS

CHERRY BUFFET, 2017   CHERRY, WALNUT PULLS   35" H x 70" W x 21" D
Wayne Delyea   Granbury, Texas   USA

Photos by Wayne Delyea

CRAIG THIBODEAU
CT FINE FURNITURE

furniture, marquetry, decorative inlay, and mechanical puzzle cabinets

(619) 981-4508
info@ctfinefurniture.com
www.ctfinefurniture.com
San Diego, California

THE MOXON VISE
RAISE YOUR WORK TO NEW HEIGHTS

by Norman Pirollo

I like the simplicity of the Moxon vise and the fact it has its origins 300 years ago. The Moxon vise design is attributed to Joseph Moxon (1627 – 1691), hydrographer to Charles II. Charles II was an English printer specialising in mathematical books and maps. Moxon's 17th century book The Art of Joinery first described the double-screw vise. The Moxon vise was documented in this historical publication as a double-screw held to a workbench top with clamps or holdfasts to facilitate certain work. In the next paragraphs I outline my reasons for making a Moxon vise and the process and detail of the build. A key reason for building a Moxon vise is that it raises a workpiece a few inches above the regular height of a workbench top. This single attribute was sufficient for me to embrace this centuries-old design. As an example, the fine sawing necessary when preparing dovetail joints will be at a more comfortable height and therefore easier to see.

Raised work aids tremendously in creating the accurate joinery in my furniture making. The portability of the Moxon vise was another appealing attribute. I could move the Moxon vise between my two large workbenches and place it on either side of each workbench. Once the task at hand is complete, it would be a straightforward exercise to remove the Moxon vise from the workbench top. The following paragraphs detail the steps involved in building a Moxon vise using a Benchcrafted hardware kit and locally sourced maple boards. The maple boards were rough-sawn and picked from my wood collection. I have had these boards in my wood pile since 1996. The original wood pile is shrinking as I develop and build new projects. Boards with pleasing grain characteristics and free of any imperfections were selected for the build.

The Benchcrafted Moxon Vise Kit along with the five boards to build the Moxon vise

The Benchcrafted Moxon vise hardware kit includes two cast handwheels, ACME-threaded screws, nuts, washers and a Crubber material to line the inside of the movable jaw. This Crubber (rubber & cork) material provides the friction and grip to keep clamped boards from sliding. The Moxon vise design can be adapted to any hardware if you so choose. I used off the shelf Benchcrafted hardware because it is well-engineered and would save me considerable time in sourcing hardware components. A view above of the solid cast Benchcrafted vise handwheels and instruction pamphlet for hardware installation. In the background are the rough-sawn maple boards originating from my wood pile. The maple boards selected had straight grain characteristics as well as being free of any flaws. I wanted the strongest and straightest boards from which to shape the fixed and movable jaws. The maple boards are wider and longer than the final dimensions. This allows me to process the boards beforehand and select which portion of the boards to trim to final dimensions.

There are a total of five boards to be processed and dimensioned. Although maple is the recommended wood for the Moxon vise build due to its strength, stability and closed-grain characteristics, a good substitute can be any other species of hardwood. Kiln-dried domestic hardwoods such as cherry, birch, oak, ash, elm or beech can be substituted. Two pairs of boards, when laminated together, comprise both the fixed and movable jaw. The fifth board forms a small table and support. Each of the 4/4 boards is a little over 1 inch thick. When two boards are laminated to create a jaw, the rough thickness will be over 2 inches. This leaves plenty of extra wood to trim the boards down to the final 1.75-inch thickness. An alternative approach is to use 8/4 lumber at 2 in. nominal thickness and work with this instead. If you have access to 8/4 or 2-inch nominal thickness hardwood, considerable time is saved since laminating is eliminated. When laminating, I was careful to orient the grain in each board opposite the other. This technique offsets any internal stresses remaining in the wood and maintains stability and straightness. The rough-sawn boards are then thickness planed and jointed.

It is critical to accurately joint and plane the inside faces of two adjoining boards. Since these two faces are glued together to create a thicker board, the surfaces need to be seamless across both their width and length. The straightness of the planed surface is tested using an accurate straightedge. This ensures that the surface is flat from end to end, across the width, and diagonally. The final thickness of each jaw will be 1.75 inches. One board is jointed and thickness planed on two faces while the other board is dressed or jointed on one face. This allows the final glued up board to have a jointed face as a reference in bringing the final thickness down to 1.75-inches.

The 1.75-inch final thickness for each jaw is optimized to the length of the ACME-threaded screw. This thickness provides adequate strength and allows maximum open throat depth using the 8-inch-long ACME-threaded screws included in the Benchcrafted hardware kit. Clamping the individual boards together to form the jaws is an intense process. Once it is determined that the jointed surfaces are straight, true and gap free, the glue-up can begin. To save time, I have all necessary clamps close by.

Depending on the glue you use, there is a set time associated with each type or brand of glue. It is critical to have all the clamps in place within the recommended set time. This eliminates any issues with thick glue lines, gaps or incorrectly glued boards. The number of clamps necessary are seen below. The rough boards are 32 inches long and 6 inches in width. Many clamps are necessary in the glue-up. I use my strongest parallel clamps for this operation. Parallel clamps distribute equal pressure along their jaws and easily handle the heavy, thick boards.

An alternative to multiple clamps is to place cauls across the length or width of the laminations. Cauls spread clamping pressure uniformly along the surface of the wood, resulting in the need for fewer clamps. If using cauls, a common technique is to create a slight convex curve in the center of the caul. The convex area ensures that the middle of the caul exerts equivalent pressure as the outside edges when clamped. If you opt to use solid 8/4 lumber in the build, I recommend using boards with rift-sawn grain orientation. Rift-sawn boards exhibit less cupping, bowing and twisting characteristics than plain-sawn wood.

Several clamps are used to clamp two large boards forming the 2 inch thick jaw lamination

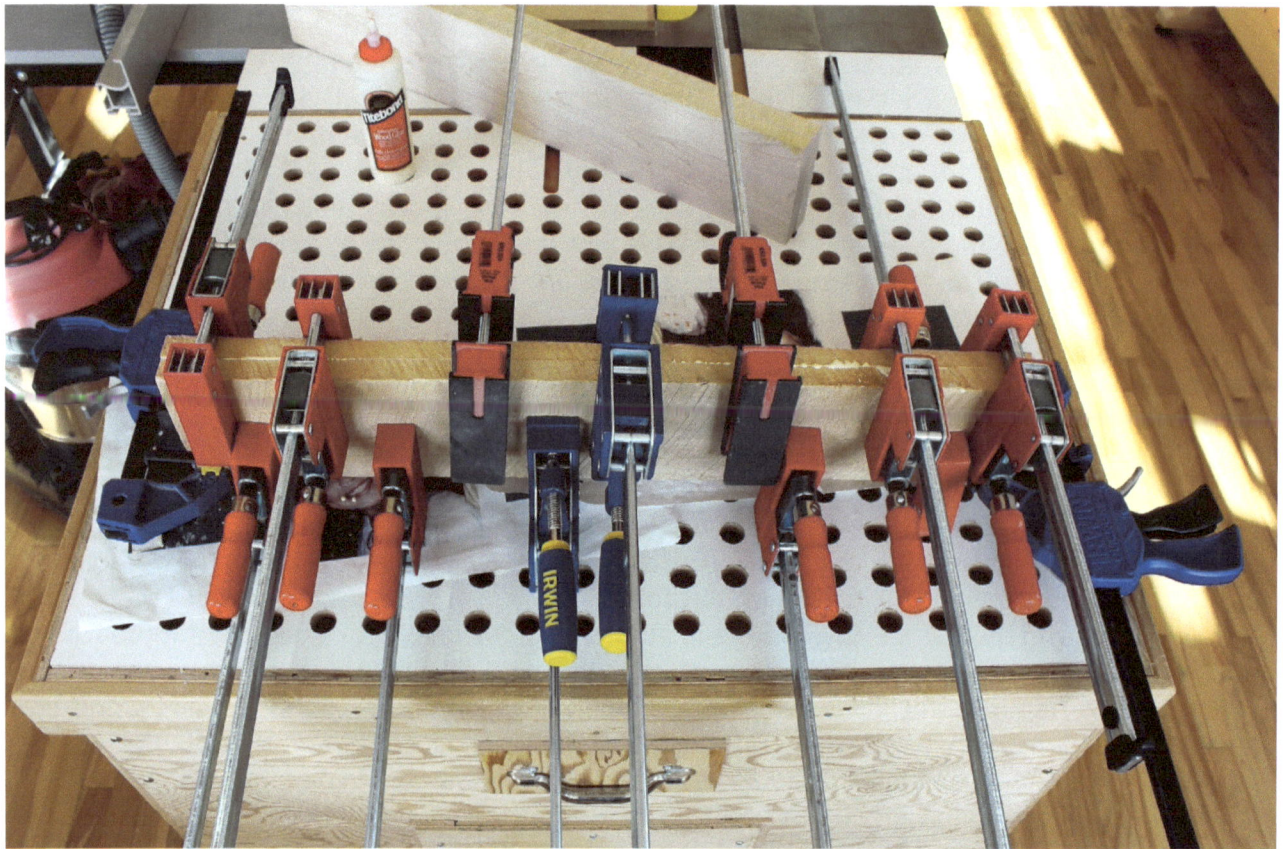

The opposing grain pattern in each of the boards composing the lamination

Rift-sawn wood has the grain running diagonally or from corner to corner if looking at an end. Rift-sawn wood is used in table or chair legs and is radially cut from a log as opposed to the tangential cuts of plain-sawn boards. Although time consuming to laminate thin boards to form a thick board, there are advantages. A thick laminated board is more stable if the boards are laminated with grain orientation opposite each other. This observation is empirical and gleaned over several years of laminating boards together.

The key is to counter the instability in one board with the other board. The laminated boards then balance each other out with swings in humidity and air temperature. In this photo, this method of lamination can be seen. The distinct growth rings opposing each other in each lamination are visible. After the glue on the pair of laminated boards has cured, the next step is to reduce the thick board down to 1.75 inches. As you recall, one outside face has already been jointed flat. This face is now the reference surface when passing the board through a thickness planer.

It is next necessary to remove 1/4 in. from the overall 2-inch thickness of the board. A few passes through a thickness planer followed by final smoothing with a hand plane accomplishes this. Approximately 1/8 inches is removed with the thickness planer. Once both outside surfaces are parallel and smooth, flip the board for a final pass on the reference surface. The board can is then handplaned to reduce the final thickness to 1.75-inches. You can optionally leave the handplaning step out and use a thickness planer to reduce the thickness of the combined lamination to an accurate 1.75 inches.

Light final passes are recommended as the thick board approaches the 1.75-inch thickness. Exercise care in running the boards through the thickness planer in the correct direction or with the grain to eliminate tearout issues. To avoid mistakes, I typically mark the correct direction along the side of the board using a pencil mark of an arrow. The final passes to bring the board down to 1.75 inches in thickness were performed using a No.7 Jointer plane. This leaves a smooth, hand planed surface. Recall, 1/8 inch was removed from the 2 in. lamination with a planer.

A hand plane is then used to reduce the final thickness of the thick wood down to 1.75 inches. Handplaning also provides an exceptionally smooth surface. There is relatively no risk of tearout using a well-tuned and adjusted hand plane such as the No. 7. Alternatively, a large No. 5 Jack plane or No. 6 Fore plane can be used to reduce the thickness of each jaw. I recommend setting the hand plane for light cuts and instead make multiple passes. This is a prudent, risk-free approach leaving a polished, tearout-free surface.

If you decide to forgo this step, use a thickness planer to reduce the lamination thickness to an accurate 1.75 inches without any snipe. With the boards comprising the front and rear jaw reduced to a 1.75-inch thickness, the next step is dimensioning each board to an accurate length and width. In this Moxon vise design, I opted for both jaws to be the same length since I will not have F-clamps attaching the vise to the workbench. Instead, holdfasts clamp the stabilizer block to the workbench. Although you can create a Moxon vise in any length from about 20 inches to 36 inches, my design calls for a length somewhere in the middle.

A 28-in. length was decided on based on the work I perform in my furniture making. I rarely have a need for a wider twin-screw vise. After finalizing the 28-inch length, 3.5 inches from either end are marked for the ACME-threaded screw location. The overall usable vise length remaining will be 20 inches. This is more than sufficient for any work I clamp to the workbench. The length and 5 1/2-inch width of each vise jaw marked and sawn using a table saw. The front or movable jaw is wider (1/8 in.) to allow for an overhang at leading edge of the workbench. The 1/8 in. overhang facilitates registration of the Moxon vise to workbench.

If modifying the design for your own work methods, determine the width of panels you most often clamp to your workbench. Ensure you give this decision plenty of thought since once cut, the vise jaws cannot be lengthened. Another consideration is the weight of the Moxon vise. By reducing the length of the vise to the size you use most often, the vise is lighter and easier to move around. In my design, these criteria received considerable thought and a 28-inch length was chosen.

Running the laminated jaw through a thickness planer to remove approx. 1/8 in.

Handplaning the surface of the laminated jaw to remove a final fraction of an inch. A few passes will accomplish this. The laminated jaws are then trimmed to size using a tablesaw as shown below. A shop-built crosscut sled is used for this operation.

In my design, these criteria received considerable thought and a 28-inch length was chosen. Since the Moxon vise is attached at the rear stabilizer block using holdfasts, a longer, notched rear jaw is eliminated. A longer, notched rear jaw would otherwise be clamped to the workbench using F-clamps. Clamping from the rear of the vise also provides a cleaner aesthetic. Next, holes are bored for the 3/4 in. ACME-threaded screws. Locations for drilling are marked on both boards. The 3/4-inch screw holes are located 3.5 in. from each end and 2.75 inches from the top. I recommend accurately marking the top and both faces of each board to avoid mistakes. Two holes in each 1.75 in. thick jaw are drilled. Each jaw is placed against the drill press fence and slid from side to side when drilling holes. The second jaw is placed against the same fence setting to ensure holes are precisely bored in both jaws. I insert a backer board between the workpiece and the drill press table. The backer board prevents blow out or splintering of the hole when the Forstner bit exits the bottom of the hole. A backer board is a sacrificial board that is flat and at least ¼ inch thick. The holes in the front jaw are slightly elongated on either side (1/16 in.) to allow for non-parallel jaw movement on irregular wood pieces.

After creating the 3/4 in. holes, I followed the Benchcrafted recommendation and elongated the holes about 1/16 in. on either side. It is critical to only elongate the holes from side to side and not from top to bottom. If the holes are instead elongated from top to bottom, the front jaw will not line up with the rear jaw and sit lower. After the 3/4 in. holes are precisely drilled to match the holes in the front jaw, the ACME-threaded screw and nut are temporarily installed in each hole of the rear jaw. Marking the mortise for the nut on the inner face of the rear jaw is next. With the screw locked with nuts on the inside and outside face of the rear jaw, I simply oriented the nut and marked its outline on the inside face of the rear jaw. The orientation of the six-sided nut is parallel to the jaw sides, as seen in the image. This step is repeated for both screw holes in the rear jaw. Since the six-sided nut is large, it makes sense to chuck a large Forstner bit (1 1/16 in.) into the drill press and remove as much wood waste as possible.

A drill press bores 3/4 in. holes used for the ACME-threaded screws and nuts

Mortise for captive six-sided nut created using bevel-edge and mortise chisels

The mortise is bored down 3/4 inches, the thickness of the nut. All that remains is to chisel out the wood forming the outline of each six-sided nut. If you do not have access to a drill press, use a drilling guide. A drilling guide is a tall block of wood with a 3/4-inch diameter hole drilled vertically through. The hole must be perpendicular to the face of the drilling guide. The guide is clamped to the jaw surface and a Forstner bit and drill are used to bore a 3/4-inch diameter hole. I use this technique to bore holes in workbench tops since the top is too large to place on a drill press table. It is critical to mortise the six-sided nut into the rear jaw to slightly below the level of the surface. This keeps the nut from interfering with clamping operations. Some trial and error is involved in creating the mortise deep enough. A small ruler fit into the mortise can be used to determine the depth and wood left to remove. Bevel-edge and mortise chisels were used to clean the mortise out. Since the jaws are hard maple, mortise chisels excel at this operation. With softer wood, I might get away with using only bevel-edge chisels.

Bevel-edge chisels were used to outline the cut and heavier mortise chisels removed the waste. This step is tedious, but the results are worth it. Having the nut completely housed is aesthetically pleasing and strong. The alternative is to create a square mortise nut and fit the nut into the mortise. This procedure is outlined in the Benchcrafted instructions. In this photo, a cleaned-up mortise is seen, as well as a mortise chisel used to hog wood out. There is trial and error in fitting the large six-sided nut to the mortise since it needs to sit below the face of the rear jaw. This operation is performed on both screw holes in the rear jaw. The recommended width of the front and rear jaws was gleaned from Benchcrafted instructions. The instructions call for a rear jaw width of 5 1/2 inches and a front jaw width of 5 5/8 inches. The extra 1/8-inch width of the front jaw allows it to overhang the edge of the workbench for alignment. The distance from the center of each screw hole to the top and outside edge of rear or fixed jaw is:

2.75 inches from top (1/2 of the width of the jaw itself @ 5.5 inches)
3.5 inches from outside edge (allows for handwheel to fit within edges)

The screw hole alignment is similar for the front jaw since the 1/8-inch portion overhanging the leading edge of the workbench sits below the surface of the workbench. In the photo below, a six-sided nut is fit into its captive mortise. The extra time spent creating accurate mortises for these nuts is well worth it. The aesthetic of seeing a nut completely housed into the surface is a sign of good craftsmanship. As well, the strength and holding power of the nut in a mortise is second to none. You can go the extra step and orient the face of the nut so two of its points are parallel to the edges of the rear jaw, as shown.

The thickness of each jaw is 1.75 inches, and the thickness of the six-sided nut itself is 3/4 inches deep. This leaves 1 inch of wood in the rear jaw between the inside and outside faces, more than enough to maintain rigidity and strength. Both six-sided nuts are fitted into the inside face of the rear, fixed jaw. This step is easily the most time consuming of the Moxon vise build, but a critical step to get right. The front and rear jaws are dimensioned to be identical in length with the front jaw slightly wider by 1/8 inch. The next step is to test fit the hardware. Once the ACME-threaded screws, large nuts and handwheels fit and function correctly, the build can resume.

The screw holes in the front jaw are elongated from side to side to allow clamping of irregular pieces of wood. Irregular clamping causes one side of the front jaw to not be parallel with the rear jaw. The extra wide screw hole allows the front, movable jaw to move freely along the screw length. This is accomplished by shifting and drilling the front jaw left or right of the main screw hole 1/16 inch on either side. The hole is bored through again with the extra 1/16-inch and precisely elongates the front jaw holes. Avoid elongating the holes in the vertical direction.

Although this step can be performed using a wood rasp by carefully gouging out the left and right sides of the 3/4 in. screw hole, I opted to use a drill press and 3/4-inch Forstner bit. The choice is yours to which method you feel comfortable with. One of two ACME-threaded screws is fitted into the rear, fixed jaw. The mortised nut and rear nut have been installed. There is not much torque necessary to lock the screw down since the front nut is captured in its mortise. The bored screw hole for the ACME-threaded screw is a little over 3/4 inch and the threaded screw is a tight fit. A second screw is installed on the opposite side of the rear, jaw and the front jaw then test-fitted to the rear jaw.

Mortise and bevel-edge chisels are used to hog out the wood for the six-sided captured nut.

Mortises for six-sided nuts complete and nuts inserted. The captured nuts sit just below the surface of the rear jaw. Below, the ACME-threaded screws are installed into the rear jaw. A large hex nut at the rear of the jaw locks the hardware assembly into place.

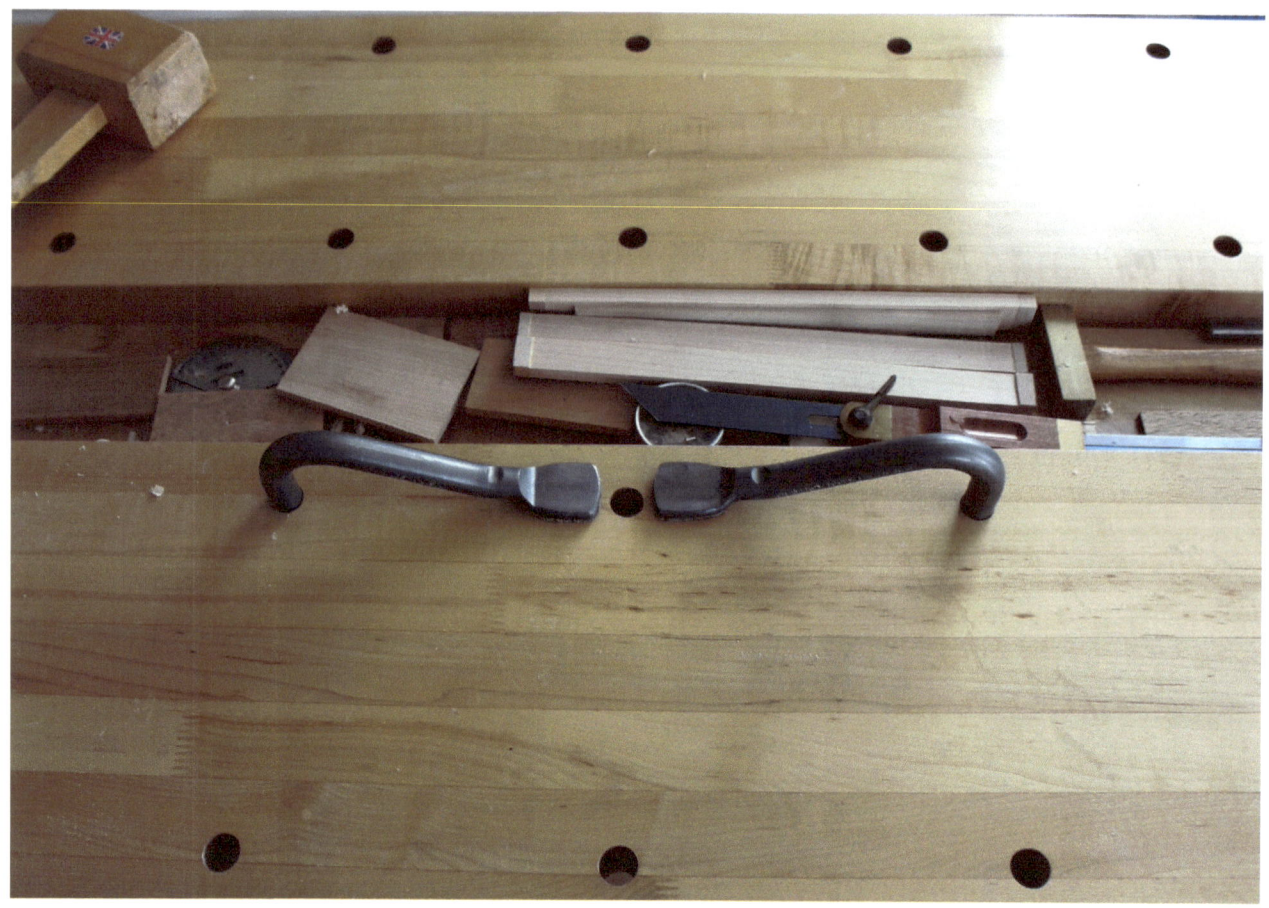

Holdfasts are inserted into dog holes of workbench top

Movement of the front jaw is tested for both parallel operation and when skewed as in irregular clamping. During this test, the rear jaw is temporarily clamped to the workbench top. The next step is to determine how large a stabilizer block is necessary to ensure the rear jaw is firmly attached to the workbench top. The stabilizer block is glued to the bottom back face of the rear jaw and keeps the Moxon vise square to the workbench. It also provides a clamping surface for the holdfasts. Above, the Gramercy holdfasts used to clamp the Moxon vise to the workbench.

I have been using Gramercy holdfasts for a while and am pleased with them. They are relatively inexpensive and perform well. I glued a small piece of Crubber liner to the bottom of each pad to increase friction and prevent the holdfasts from slipping while clamping the Moxon vise. I opted for holdfasts rather than the alternative of using bar clamps at either side of the Moxon vise. The holdfasts provide a cleaner aesthetic. Due to the layout of the dog holes in my workbenches, using holdfasts made more sense.

By using holdfasts at the rear, the extra length of the rear jaw is eliminated. Normally, it is recommended to have the rear jaw a few inches wider at each side to allow for an F-clamp. Instead, this design calls for the front and rear jaws to be similar in length. It should be noted that most Moxon vise configurations are pre-existing and derivative of one another. I simply adapted an existing design to my own workbench and work methods. After all, the original Moxon vise illustration dates from the late 1700's.

Shown at right, an overhead view of the almost completed Moxon vise before the addition of small table and support. Laminations forming the front and rear jaws are seen with stabilizer block also visible. The stabilizer block is glued to the rear jaw and squares the vise to the workbench top. It also provides a clamping surface for the holdfasts. Holdfast pads are aligned with the outside edges of the stabilizer block. The stabilizer block is customized to your own workbench. A series of dog holes might need to be bored in your workbench top for the holdfasts. In this design, an existing row of dog holes in the center of the workbench top is used.

Once the stabilizer block is glued to the bottom of the rear jaw, it is critical to keep all bottom surfaces of the vise flush with each other and square to the jaw faces. I recommend temporarily installing the Moxon vise to the front edge of your workbench using F-clamps or bar clamps. With the vise clamped in place, you can measure the distance from the top of the stabilizer bar to where the holdfasts are inserted. This will be the location of the dog holes necessary in your workbench. I use Gramercy holdfasts in this build and have customized the Moxon vise to work within this constraint.

Another brand of holdfast will have a different size and arm length. The Moxon vise with ACME-threaded screws is attached to the workbench top. After bolting down the screws through the rear six-sided nuts, a square is used to ensure each ACME-threaded screw is perpendicular to the face. A small extension table is also seen. The table extension can be added later after ensuring that clamping to the workbench top is successful. In normal operation, the front jaw is tightened against the rear jaw and the vise is set against the edge of the workbench. Since the front jaw sits below the surface of the workbench top by 1/8 inch, this technique registers the vise to the workbench top.

In the photo on the next page, the 1/8-inch overhang of the front jaw is seen. Creating the front jaw 1/8-inch wider, establishes this overhang. The overhang registers the Moxon vise to the workbench top. Once the front jaw is locked to the rear jaw, the Moxon vise is placed against the leading edge of the workbench top and the holdfasts clamped down. This small detail ensures that the Moxon vise is aligned with the workbench edge.

Since the vise is portable, the otherwise lengthy process of registering it with the workbench edge would soon become a chore. Also shown are the opposing grain orientations in both the fixed and movable jaw. Opposing grain orientation was discussed in an earlier step. Opposing grain orientation provides stability and balance. The movement of each laminated board is countered by the opposite board. Later, a rear view of the Moxon vise with table extension added, vertical table support will be shown. All vise components are oriented with grain in the same direction or long-grain to long-grain. This prevents any long-grain to short-grain issues. In this configuration, the rear nuts are accessible if the vise needs to be disassembled.

Top view of Moxon vise without additional table and support at rear

Wider front jaw sitting below workbench surface, registering closed vise to workbench top

The front jaw is lined with the rubber and cork material Crubber provided in the Benchcrafted hardware kit. A sheet of Crubber was glued on using wood glue, then uniformly clamped down, and trimmed to size once cured. The holdfasts can be left permanently on the workbench and swung into place when clamping the Moxon vise to the workbench top. An earlier image shows the holdfasts aligned parallel to the workbench top. The height of the Moxon vise is 5 1/2 inches. I used the Benchcrafted provided guideline as a basis for selecting the dimensions for this vise.

The height suffices to allow for some clearance of the handwheels on the face of the front jaw. The height at 5 1/2 inches keeps the width of the jaws to a minimum while maintaining a smooth, obstruction-free operation of the handwheels. The completed Moxon vise seen on the next page with Crubber material applied to the inside of the front jaw. Handwheels are installed and tested. The extension table is supported along its width and length by supporting wood beneath the table.

This enables pounding on the table when chopping dovetails using a mallet and chisel. The vise can be located anywhere on the workbench where two dog holes are available in the center row as shown. The Moxon vise is not light, but not heavy enough to discourage portability. I prefer the added mass of dense maple hardwood. The extra weight mitigates any blows delivered through the table and keeps the vise firmly attached to the workbench surface. Most hardwoods can be used to build the Moxon vise. Maple was selected since it has a tight, closed grain and is easy to work with hand tools.

At right, front view of completed Moxon vise. The outside edges of the jaws are chamfered to eliminate sharp edges. A small block plane is used for this task with a few passes on each long edge and the ends. I count the number of passes to ensure that the chamfers are uniform in appearance. Only the outside edges of both jaws and table components are chamfered. The area in and around where the jaws meet is left with crisp, square handplaned edges.

Leaving handplaned edges on the inside faces of the jaws maintains uniform, square edges where the front and rear jaw meet. On the next page,, a side view of the completed Moxon vise with extension table and support. The massive stabilizer block is seen where holdfasts clamp the vise to the workbench top. Directly behind the stabilizer is the vertical support for the table. The table support is shorter than the stabilizer to allow holdfast pads to access the top of the stabilizer block. In the photo, the table is supported along its width and length by the vertical support. This enables me to pound on the table when chopping out dovetails using a chisel and mallet.

This Moxon vise design is customized for this workbench and location of the center dog holes. The Gramercy holdfast arm length has been factored into this. There is an allowance for the holdfasts to be swung in either direction if the Moxon vise is offset left or right of the dog holes. When adapting to your own workbench, a series of dog holes a few inches from the rear of the Moxon vise is necessary to clamp the vise down. This workbench is a Veritas model with pre-drilled dog holes along both sides of the center.

The Moxon vise is stored on its side when not in use. The profile of the vise is under 6 inches, so it can be unobtrusively placed along a wall. Storing on its side also makes use of the square area behind the table. The Moxon vise stored on its side is shown later along with a strip at rear of the vise to keep the vise perpendicular when vertical. The hand wheels face up when the vise is stored against a wall. Shown on the next pages is the rear view of the Moxon vise with components of the table and vertical support. The table support is shorter in length than the stabilizer block to allow for the holdfast pads.

Also visible is a square block of wood directly below the leading edge of the table glued to the rear jaw. This additional block of wood or filler supports the table at this edge for mallet work. The large rear nut is also accessible in this configuration. I rarely work with very large panels and this table size is more than wide enough for my needs. In your design, you can substitute a wider or longer table, depending on the work you intend to perform on the Moxon vise. The Moxon vise design is configurable in this regard.

Photo of Moxon vise clamped to a workbench top. Holdfasts are unobtrusive at rear

Photo of rear of Moxon vise with additional table support beneath table

Ensure the table is adequately supported if pounding with a mallet is a part of your work methods. When building your Moxon vise, use either 8/4 or 2-inch nominal hardwood or laminate (2) 4/4 or 1-inch boards together to create each jaw. I opted for laminated boards since I had considerable 4/4 maple boards on hand. If using a solid 8/4 board, ensure the grain orientation is straight and preferably rift-sawn. Plainsawn boards can cup if not kiln-dried to the correct moisture level.

Plainsawn boards are also susceptible to changes in humidity and temperature. If using 8/4 or 2-inch stock, instead of tangentially oriented plain-sawn boards, use rift-sawn or quarter-sawn boards. Rift-sawn or quarter-sawn boards are dimensionally stable and preferred. If laminating (2) plainsawn boards together, use the opposing grain technique described earlier. This ensures the thick jaws maintain equilibrium and are stable during moisture changes in your workshop space. Above, the completed Moxon vise with table extension components attached.

In an alternative design, the table can be extended along its length and width. I opted for this configuration to save on weight and to provide a small table surface for tasks most often performed. This configuration allows access to the ACME-threaded screws and rear nuts as well as freedom of movement of holdfasts. Over time, I intend to work with this design and determine if improvements are necessary. Although this Moxon vise design is universal, configure your vise to the work performed at your workbench.

Shown, a detailed view of the ACME screw, and rear nut in the fixed jaw. The holdfast and pad that grip the rear stabilizer block are also visible. The holdfasts swing into position to clamp the Moxon vise down. When released, the holdfasts swing back to a less obtrusive position as shown earlier. The holdfasts can also be removed and used elsewhere. Crubber has been fixed to the inside face of the movable jaw. Applying this material to the jaw face is straightforward using wood glue. I applied uniform clamping across the surface of the wood for two hours.

Afterwards, the extra material was trimmed down to the four edges of the front jaw using a sharp knife. Afterwards, the extra material was trimmed down to the four edges of the front jaw using a sharp knife. As a final step, a 3/8-inch thick extension strip is applied to the rear bottom of the table support as shown in the image below and on the next page. This extension strip extends the bottom to the same depth as the table itself. When the Moxon vise is mounted on its side as shown on next page, it will be perfectly vertical against a wall.

The 3/8-inch thick extension strip is necessary since the table extends past the table support a distance of 3/8-inches. With the extension strip applied to the lower back as shown, the Moxon vise will be perfectly vertical in orientation. The view shows the bottom of the Moxon vise where the extension strip is applied to the lower side of the table support. I was pleasantly surprised to find out how little space the Moxon vise occupied when placed against a wall. Since hard maple was used in this build, this Moxon vise is not light, due to the hardwoods and weight of the cast hardware. The advantage is that the Moxon vise is stable and strong.

With the Moxon vise, I can now work at a comfortable height without stooping down to the work. This stance is very beneficial when sawing dovetails and for detail work. The additional table at the rear provides a platform for marking and chisel work performed on a workpiece. You can modify the design to suit your work methods and the scale of your work. This shop-built Moxon vise is derivative and introduces a few new features. The vise uses current hardware and is a modern adaptation of a centuries old, time-proven design.

There is a resurgence of interest in early woodworking techniques, processes and workbench equipment. The Moxon vise is an excellent example of how everything old is new again. Your back and posture will thank you after having used the Moxon vise for a while. Being hunched over for long periods can affect your posture and cause all sorts of back issues. I can also see how it will benefit a taller woodworker. Of course, you can customize the Moxon vise to adapt to your workbench. So go ahead and raise your work to new heights with a Moxon vise. The vise will be a welcome addition to my furniture making studio!

Photo of rear of Moxon vise with extra hardwood strip, table and table support

Rear view of completed Moxon vise with addition of hardwood strip to keep the vise square when placed vertically against a wall as shown below.

Various measuring instruments used in woodworking and furniture making. Image framed with two block planes, a low angle and standard angle. The block planes are intrinsic to hand work and very versatile in their application. Center finder tool, measuring tool, various squares, sliding bevel gauge, folding rule, beading tools, depth gauge are seen above.

P̲O̲P̲ MAKING THE CASE FOR LAMINATION
by Jan Lennon

Incorporate lamination and veneer into your furniture design and raise it to a new level of uniqueness. Lamination and veneer adds character to the aesthetic. Learn how to create curved work through the lamination process and vacuum veneering.

Photo by Jan Lennon

Introduction

When producing a curved section or item in wood there are several different approaches that can be considered – should the piece be shaped from solid wood, steam bent, or laminated from several layers of solid wood, plywood and/or veneer? Each method has its advantages and drawbacks but, when compared to the alternative methods available, lamination certainly has several points in its favor.

The strength of the section created with lamination is a definite plus to those wanting to create a slim profile without compromising on structural integrity. Carving or shaping a curve from solid wood means that at some point along the curve short grain will come into play and be required to take some of the load. This is less than ideal and, depending on the extremity of the curve, can be too weak to bear the requisite load or pressure without breaking. In contrast, creating the same section by bending and gluing several thin layers of solid or plywood to get the same effect results in a piece where the long grain runs continuously around the curve. This provides a surprising amount of strength for a relatively small thickness. The addition of layers of glue also adds strength to the curve. Simply put, unless the curve is relatively shallow, a lamination is stronger than solid.

"Aha", I hear you say, "but solid wood can be steam bent to produce the same result!" This is true and in some cases, considering the style of the piece being made, can be the most appropriate method to use. But in many situations, style permitting, lamination still has the upper hand over steambending.

Where dimensional accuracy is of high importance, laminated sections are undeniably more predictable and accurate than steam bent sections. An amount of spring back is almost a certainty with steam bending and can be considerable in tighter radii or thicker sections of wood. This is difficult to predict accurately and also varies depending on species of wood, grain pattern and how the stock has been dried and processed. In comparison, although some laminations can experience a slight amount of spring back, this is dependent only on a few factors, such as thickness of layers and design of the former which can be calculated for. Steambending can also introduce compression folds into the inner curve of tighter bends and introduce some tension into the section which can affect the stability of the final piece.

The cost and material efficiency of choosing to laminate can also sway to the maker as follows. Facing a plywood section with veneer can allow the maker to use a burr, or unusual species without the expense of buying the same in solid. More importantly, it should be taken into consideration that veneer harvested from one tree can be used in tens or hundreds of projects as opposed to the same in solid. So if such a grain or species is used, veneer can be the more environmentally responsible way to include it.

The consistent repeatability of laminated sections is also a considerable advantage if you consider making more than one of the item or section. This makes it ideal for small batch production, or for use in a piece where symmetry is of the utmost importance.

A background to lamination techniques

The lamination itself can also be done in several different ways. Traditionally, sections with a curve along one direction can be made accurately and repeatedly using a pair of formers, male and female. In some cases, multiple formers are used for complicated pieces. The layers to be laminated are pressed between the formers, pressure applied and the piece left to dry.

A more free-form curve in two directions can be made with a smaller cross section but to considerable length by applying the glue to thin layers of wood, fixing the position at either end and applying pressure in between with a series of clamps and cauls, or by wrapping tightly with a bicycle tube inner.

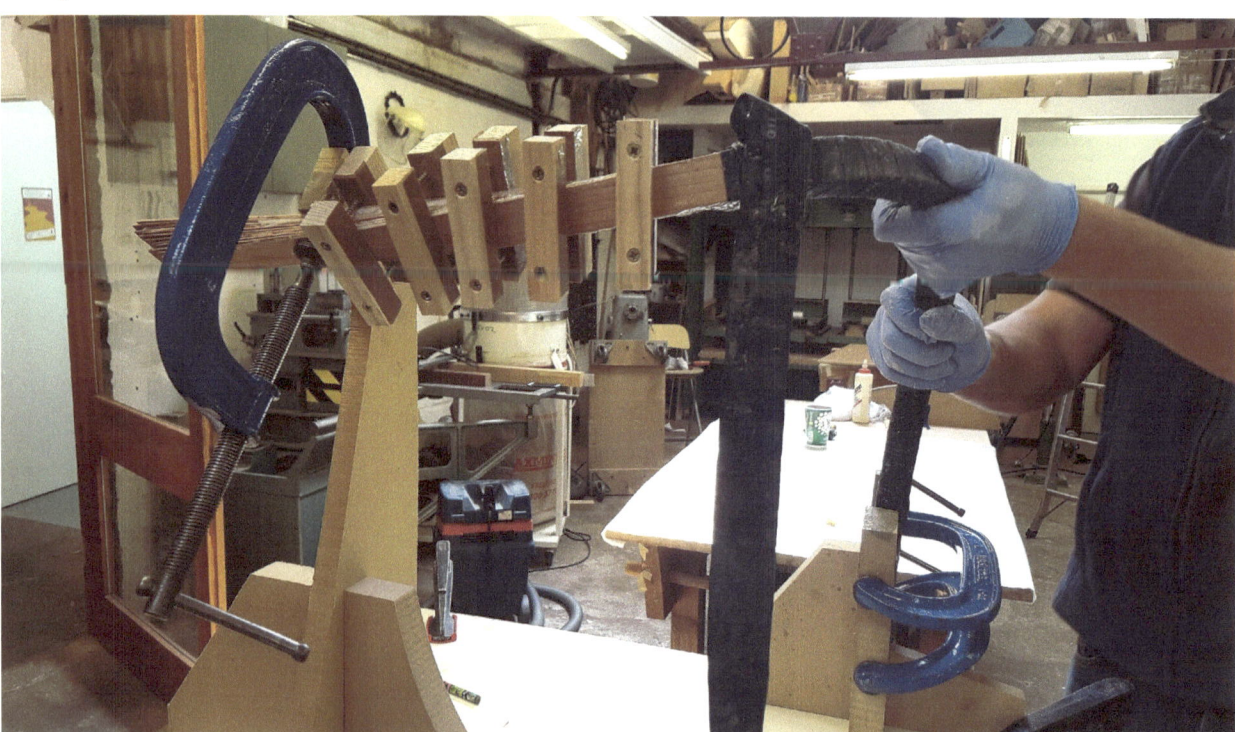

All of these methods are tried and tested and produce very good results. The rest of this article, however, will focus on laminating using a vacuum press. This is the method whereby the layers to be laminated are placed over a male former which is then placed into a reusable thick plastic bag. The bag is sealed and a vacuum pump attached.

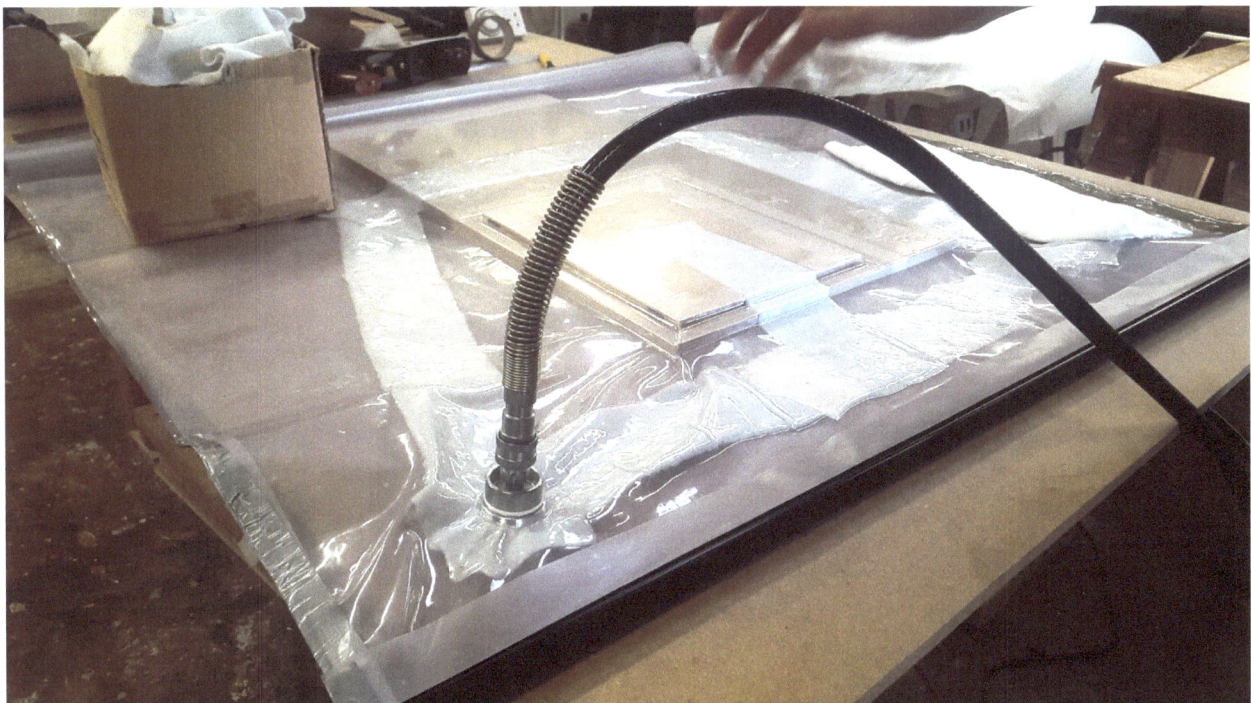

The pressure applied when the air is pumped out of the bag is about 10 tonnes per square metre (15psi) and is enough to produce a very good and repeatable result. The application of uniform pressure over the workpiece, for a well-designed former, removes the difficulty this can pose with other methods.

For single items and small batch production it has the advantage over the traditional two-former process in that only a male former needs to be made. This is considerably cheaper, quicker and easier to engineer than manufacturing corresponding male and female formers.

The equipment involved in using a vacuum press is quite pricey, but if you intend to do quite a few laminations during your woodworking life, then it is an economical investment and space saver in the long run as it can also be used for all of your veneering work and packed away when not in use.

In the following discussion, flexiply or bendy ply refers to thin 3-ply 1.5mm birch plywood with the characteristic of bending easily. This is often referred to as aircraft plywood or aeroply.

Laminating curved sections using the vacuum press
The Process
Designing the laminated section

When designing the piece to be laminated, there are several factors which should be taken into account.

1. Curve direction and material: Most veneers prefer to bend in one direction only at any given point and the same applies to thin (1.5mm) birch plywood/ aeroply and thin layers of solid wood. That's not to say that a compound curved surface is not possible with this method, but it is very much a matter of careful design and probably a few trials – caveat maker! For most projects, and for the purpose of this article, it is more useful to consider a one directional curve, several of which can be joined together at another point to create a surface with a compound curve.

2. Under-hangs: Areas which curve under the former, should also be avoided as these are points where pockets of air can get trapped in the bag and so pressure cannot be uniformly and adequately applied.

3. Former construction: Try not to necessitate the use of a former that is needlessly difficult to prepare or requires the use of expensive processes, such as use of a 5 axis CNC, unless the project calls for and warrants the complication.

4. Material usage: Aeroply and thin solid layers will bend in one direction only and layers of veneers should generally also be oriented with the same grain direction. So during the planning stage, it is good practice if you can plan how you will lay out out the material for cutting most efficiently.

5. Finishing the lamination: It is good to plan in advance how the lamination will be trimmed and treated after forming as this may cause you to change some details of the design.

Once the section is designed, the material can be prepared. When pre-cutting the layers, it is good to include an allowance, or shoulder, of 2-4mm around the entire layer. Glue can cause a little bit of slippage during glue up and this gives you enough of a "safety zone" to trim the final piece to size. Cut one extra layer of the aeroply with an extra shoulder of 4mm around all edges and set this aside.

Constructing the Former

A former can be made from any material which will take the compression forces applied by the vacuum without deforming. There are companies which can manufacture these to your specification from dense form or MDF by using a hot wire or CNC machine. Or it may suit your design to turn one on a lathe and cut down to the section required. The method chosen for use here is one which can be made easily enough in the workshop and adapted to many different designs.

The first step is to create a side view template of the former from sheet material. Use a sheet thickness that the bearing of a router trimming cutter can run along – I find that 9mm MDF is perfect for this job. Lay aside enough decorative veneer to skin the former later. This can be any veneer you have at hand. Measure the thickness of this veneer.

The rest of the former will follow this template so it is worth spending the time here to make sure that it is as accurate to the inner curve of the piece being made as is practicable. Subtract the thickness of the skinning veneer from the curve.

Add at least 75mm to the base of the former to allow the vacuum bag to pull into the edge and around 10mm each side to the width. Once this is ready the template can be traced around and transferred to the sheet material that will be used to construct the former. This could be MDF or chipboard, whatever is cheapest or closest at hand – the last few formers I made were repurposed from a Swedish flat pack wardrobe that had fallen apart and which I had cannibalized for parts. This had the advantage of being free, close at hand and saved me throwing it on the rubbish heap.

Once the layers have been roughly band sawn out, the template can be fixed to the first layer using panel pins and trimmed to size. The template is removed, the "prime" layer is then screwed to the next roughed out layer and the trimming is repeated. Successive layers are added and trimmed until the requisite width has been reached. If the width is considerable, every second layer can be a hollow "edge only" layer made from lumber or sheet material offcuts. This will lighten the former and save on materials whilst maintaining adequate strength in the structure.

When finished, run down the edges of the former with sandpaper to take the arris (sharp edges) off as sharp edges can damage the vacuum bag. Cover the top of the former (surface that will be used to laminate the piece) with the veneer you set aside earlier and tape down at the edges. This helps smooth out the former and prevents dust or bits of chipboard from being glued to the lamination.

Cover this, in turn, with a layer of thick plastic sheeting (I found that cutting up a dust collector bag does a pretty good job). The plastic stops the lamination from sticking to the former. Cut another layer to drape over the top of the layers being laminated for the same reason and set aside.

There are two more items you need to prepare before you can start setting up for glue up. Firstly, you will need some sort of top board to cover the lamination and help the bag settle evenly over the piece. This needs to be flexible enough to follow the curve of the former but doesn't need to have any great strength. Thin hardboard or aeroply (very thin 3-ply birch plywood) is a good choice. This is what the extra layer of aeroply that you cut earlier will now be used for. The extra 4mm is to ensure that all parts of the lamination are covered by the board in case of slippage. The amount is not enough to cause the overhang issues discussed earlier. Remove the arris (sharp edge) on this board also.

Finally, you will need a base board to place in the bag to prevent the bag from pulling up around the former and bunching. This should be relatively thick (at least 12mm) and larger than the former base by at least 25%. Remove the arris (sharp edges) on this also and cover with some thin plastic sheeting – decorator's sheeting is an economical choice and always useful to have in a workshop.

Gluing Up

A dry run is always a good idea before final glue up. But as it would only be repeating information, we'll go straight to setting up and gluing up. Lay out the vacuum bag on a flat surface and place the plastic covered base board inside. Surround the edges of the base board with strips of wool breather fabric. You should have more breather fabric close at hand for when you place the former inside. The breather fabric will allow the pump to continue to pull the plastic bag down onto the piece without self-sealing against the edges of the board or former. Everything should be now ready for gluing up. It's good to try and think ahead and have anything that you might need close at hand as you'll need to move pretty quickly once the glue is on the layers.

Glue choice for any process seems to always be a point of debate amongst woodworkers, but for laminations I would certainly avoid the use of any PVA or "yellow" glues like Titebond. These glues work brilliantly for joinery but have a certain amount of cold creep (movement or stretching when dry) which can cause your laminations to spring back, delaminate or just fail altogether. Instead, a resin glue which has little or no creep is preferable. Powdered resins such as Cascamite, Urea Formaldehyde resin glues such as Prefere 4152 or, for very heavy duty items or items with more materials than wood being used, an epoxy resin such as West Systems can be considered.

Apply an even layer of glue about half a millimeter thick to all but the top layer to be laminated using a roller or spreader. It can be easier to lay the layers all out, edge tape them down and apply glue to all of them at once. Then stack the layers and lay the top layer on. To stop the layers from sliding too unnecessarily in the bag, you can tape the sides loosely with a piece of veneer tape. Be careful to do this on edges that will not need to stretch over the former only.

Applying glue to laminate layers using a glue roller

Place the stack on the former and, again, tape down at the apex to hold it in place. Drape this with the plastic layer, place the topping board on top and, again, tape this down.

The whole lot is now ready to go into the bag. Once it's sitting pretty centrally on the baseboard you can drape the former lengthwise with the extra breather fabric and trail this down to sit under the pump valve. This is crucial as it creates a link between the former and the vacuum pump without which the laminated section will quite probably be flawed if not ruined. I'd even suggest folding the fabric in two under the valve to give it a little more suction power.

The bag can now be sealed and the pump connected – how this is done will depend on the model vacuum pump being used. The pump is now turned on and the air is being evacuated from the bag,

This is a good time to use your hands to smooth the bag down over the piece and pull out any sharp creases or bunching that might be appearing.

The pump should reach 15psi within a few minutes. If this is not happening it will need to be remedied quickly. To find any leaks or unsealed areas, turn off the pump and listen carefully to locate any hissing sounds. Some duct tape should work to seal any leaks temporarily. If you can seal the leaks before the glue starts to go off, the lamination will not be affected.

The pump should be set for somewhere between 6-8 hours to allow the glue to set properly. As the noise can be pretty nerve jangling, my preferred option is to set it on a timer last thing in the evening or when machines will be running.

This should result in a nicely laminated section and a well-deserved pat on the back. All that's left to do now is to trim to size, attach any lippings or inset and place back in the bag one more time to laminate the inner and outer face veneers.

Once you've completed your first lamination this way a world of possibilities can open up using these techniques. It really is a very versatile method of creating a curved piece and the feeling when you open the bag and take the completed lamination off of the former is just like opening a lovely gift.

Jan Lennon is a furniture maker located in the United Kingdom. Her furniture combines traditional hand skills with contemporary manufacturing techniques to produce beautiful bespoke furniture with a modern flair.

Photo by Jan Lennon

www.janlennon.co.uk
+44 (0)77 2974 6962

info@janlennon.co.uk
@janlennonfurniture

Opposite Page
MEALA CONSOLE / DRESSING TABLE (DETAIL), 2017
BLACK WALNUT, OLIVE ASH, MDF, FLEXIPLY
798mm H x 470mm W x1208mm L
Jan Lennon United Kingdom

SIX STRATEGIES TO IMPROVE YOUR SHARPENING AND WOODWORKING

by Brian Greene

Yes, another article on sharpening. Bear with me; I think you'll like this one!

In the age before widespread mass communications, woodworking and other crafts were the domain of specialists, for the most part those who learned their craft as apprentices who typically started at a young age. Non-professional or hobbyist woodworking was encouraged by the post WWII DIY movement and the advent of shorter work weeks (more leisure time), the introduction of consumer grade power tools and the availability of information, mostly in the form of magazines, aimed at consumers. Of course, the availability of information has simply exploded in the past decade. Now anyone can do anything, almost.

What hasn't changed is that this is a complex and technical craft. Those who are serious in their endeavors to be good woodworkers, or better woodworkers, are faced with the daunting challenge of constantly learning new technical skills. It could easily be a lifelong pursuit. For those new to the craft it must seem overwhelming. My advice for beginners is to focus, as well as you can, on developing habits around core skills related to what you want to accomplish. You want to maximize your learning in a way that increases the joys and lessens the frustrations. Marking and measuring, sawing accurately, facility with a chisel are examples of core skills.

Sharpening is one of those core skills and the focus of this article. What I have to say, as you will see, is applicable to many other skill areas.

Sharpening is often called a gateway skill. While essential, in my opinion, the good news is that sharpening does not need to be very difficult, even if it never fully becomes fun!

In this article I want to offer some advice based on my experience as a woodworker, teacher and writer and as one who has studied sharpening rather closely. Advice that I hope cuts to the core of why woodworkers fail to become good sharpeners; or, to state the point more positively, advice that I hope will save you a pile of frustration and guide you to becoming a better sharpener and a better woodworker.

The professional woodworkers I know, at least those who use hand tools regularly and well, take sharpening for granted. There are lots of reasons for that. Obviously, they sharpen a lot and they've been doing it for a long time. Their methods are simple, straightforward and fast. They typically reflect the traditional techniques they were taught, methods that emphasized not wasting time on non-revenue generating tasks. Many amateurs I've encountered over the years follow their lead. Unfortunately, many others tend to make sharpening more complicated and stressful than it needs to be.

I think there are a number of things that amateur woodworkers can do to make the process less stressful and more productive. In so doing it is my hope they may come to see sharpening as a positive experience and do it often enough that it becomes an intuitive part of their daily workflow. This is my main concern.

My approach to teaching and writing about sharpening is simple: I believe that to become a better woodworker, you must become a better sharpener. There are two parts to this:

1. That woodworkers embrace sharpening and do it. Sharpening must become intuitive in order to be efficient. This is really the only goal and you can't avoid it.

2. We have never had so many options and so much literature on the subject. That's good and bad. Understanding the fundamentals is critical so that you can make informed decisions about both the techniques and the tools you will incorporate into your workflow as well as set realistic expectations about the results.

How people sharpen doesn't really concern me. I don't care much about your method or stones you use so long as you get your tools sharp.

There are lots of options and most of them work very well. While there are really no wrong choices, you should bear in mind that every choice entails some sort of compromise. (For example: Heavy or light; fast or slow; low versus high maintenance; speed versus cost.) Seek advice from others or take a class so you can try out various bits of equipment.

Before I outline the six positive steps that woodworkers can utilize to improve their sharpening, I want to point out why I believe people fail to become good sharpeners.

1. Lack of practice; not putting in the time.

2. Lack of confidence and/or an inability to make decisions for fear of making a mistake.

3. Too much focus on optimizing perfection instead of on getting tools sharp quickly. That is to say, not understanding the concept of 'good enough'.

4. Lack of good instruction, role models, etc.; someone who can teach, observe, critique and give advice.

My six strategies address these issues in ways that are practical. There is probably something here for everyone. That's my hope anyway. This list is not intended to teach you how to sharpen. I'm presuming you have already started down the path.

#1 -- Change your attitude

• There's a Japanese saying that the wise woodworker doesn't wait until the tools are dull before sharpening; he or she sharpens when they know the tools can be made better. Make sharpening a proactive, positive experience instead of a negative one. You'll be much further ahead.

• Become the woodworker who sharpens his or her tools when you know you can make them better.

• Be realistic. Want to use hand tools at a high level? Sharpening is essential. In some circles sharpening really well is a given.

• Take this seriously. Show up. Have routines that work. Put in the time. The tools won't sharpen themselves.

#2 -- Visualize

• Understand what sharp is.

• Understand what sharp tools can do. Have someone show you.

• Make decisions. Set goals. Sharp is relative to the work at hand. Not everyone needs to sharpen at extremely high levels.

• Not every tool for every job needs to be sharpened to the highest level. Not understanding the notion of 'good enough' can be incredibly inefficient. The tool that's 'good enough' may not be perfect so long as it's adequate for the task at hand.

#3 – Understand Fundamentals

• You need to know what you are doing. A little sharpening theory will help you modify your methods to suit a new situation. Take a class. Books on sharpening by Leonard Lee and Ron Hock are the industry bibles. Christopher Schwarz wrote a book on Handplanes that has 40 pages on sharpening.

• There are many acceptable methods. All of them work; some 'better' than others. Any significant differences usually relate to convenience, speed and cost. There are compromises when we make equipment choices. Do your research. Seek advice. Remember that most people do most things a little bit differently. You can start by copying someone you trust and, over time, modify the methodology to make it your own.

• Eliminate drudgery. Get some kind of grinder or, at the very least, a coarse diamond plate.

• Understand the purpose of primary and micro bevels. Use wire edges (burrs) properly.

• Don't waste your time perfecting the polish on the primary bevel. Leave it as it came from the grinder. It never touches wood. Focus your attention on the micro bevel.

• If you are using waterstones, make sure to regularly lap them flat. How often? Every 5-10 minutes of use works for me.

#4 -- Manage your expectations

• Old, abused tools will be tough to restore and will likely never give the same results as new, quality tools.? Well cared for old tools can be real gems and save a lot of money. If you want to go the old tool route you will need to educate yourself and understand that there are few certainties. New tools are a more certain thing but with a higher price. Does your work run more to carpentry or do you expect to be doing fine dovetails in hardwood? Your needs will vary.

• Be very wary of the tool pushers who would have you believe that you must have the latest this or that. There is actually very little that is truly new.

#5 -- Master one Technique

• Make decisions and pick a system that's effective, fast, convenient and works for you.

• Understand the pros and cons of your equipment.

• Sharpen often; stick with it. You will not master anything if you don't do it.

• If you are just starting and/or don't sharpen much, you should probably use a honing guide. But do not assume that a honing guide is necessary to become a good sharpener or that it will make you a better sharpener. Only time can do that. Generations of craftsmen did just fine without honing guides. Many still do. Of course, you have to learn to sharpen freehand anyway because for some tools, you have no choice.

• When faced with choices I recommend O1 steel over harder or tougher options unless, of course, a lot of your work will be in abrasive hardwoods. Ignore the promise of longer edge retention and sharpen more often. It's good for you!

• Don't forget to enjoy what you are doing! When you look at this as a positive part of woodworking, it will cease to be the chore you dread.

#6 -- Practice

• Do It! Sharpen often. Evaluate your progress. Keep trying. Learn. Own it! Make it a very deliberative process.

• Refine your methodology. Make it instinctive. When it's instinctive you won't hesitate. You'll get faster. Your tools will perform better and so will you.

• Don't over-think details that are more or less irrelevant. Remember the notion of 'good enough'.

• Touch up frequently and your tools will always be sharp. The more often you sharpen the less you sharpen.

• Regular practice is essential to developing and maintaining fine motor control as well as fine tuning your awareness of the small things that really matter.

• Practice is also important for enhancing your skills; for challenging yourself to take it to another level; to get faster; to make it more instinctive. If you are challenging yourself in other areas of woodworking, for example, ever finer dovetails, then your sharpening will have to be enhanced to keep up with your new requirements.

Learning to be a good sharpener is akin to becoming a good dovetailer or a good anything. It won't happen by itself. When you've put in the time, paid your dues and become fairly good it will be a huge confidence booster. Many who come to woodworking in middle age following a career doing other things struggle. They struggle because they tend to process things according to the norms and experience built up over a lifetime of doing other things. It seems like starting over again. Our ability to learn and, to make the transition from one world to another, can be frustrating. We don't have the patience we used to. Go easy on yourself. You can do it! It will come!

Look on the bright side. When you start sharpening well you'll always have sharp tools. When your tools are sharp you'll become a better woodworker!

Brian Greene is a writer and self-taught furniture maker. He has been teaching and demonstrating sharpening for over ten years and has written two magazine articles explaining his methods. He lives in Ottawa, Ontario Canada

Various measuring and squaring instruments used in woodworking and furniture making. Image framed with two traditional wood try squares. Center finder tool, beading tools, various squares, depth gauge, sliding bevel gauge, and measuring instruments shown.

Darrell Peart in his furniture making studio

DARRELL PEART
GREENE & GREENE

by Norman Pirollo

A candid conversation with Darrell Peart reveals his background and the inspiration for his exceptional one of a kind Greene and Green styled furniture pieces. Discover more about his journey from his teen age years to highly sought after furniture designer, maker.

From humble beginnings, one is immediately drawn to the woodworking passion that Darrell Peart exudes. With a woodworking career that spans decades, his woodworking drive and enthusiasm have remained the same, if not grown. Decades of woodworking have provided him an extensive background in high-end furniture making. Darrell can be considered a veteran woodworker, having invested time in custom furniture shops to eventually strike out on his own as a furniture maker. Darrell Peart identifies with the Arts & Crafts genre of furniture, specifically Greene & Greene style pieces. Having embraced Greene & Greene, his reputation is synonymous with this style. Although influenced by the Arts & Crafts movement, his work has taken on its own life with new and unique designs.

Peart embraces the timeless elements of Greene & Greene in his unique furniture designs. He combines tradition and innovation in his work. Darrell Peart has established his own voice and identity in the furniture making world. His work has been shown nationally. Peart is a prolific furniture maker today as well as being an educator and writer. He writes and lectures about topics that are precious to him, namely the history of Greene & Greene, woodworking and furniture design. Exploring new furniture designs is where his current passion lies. Through his teaching, he has no qualms in sharing his extensive knowledge with aspiring woodworkers. The following questions were put to Darrell to shed more light on this expert craftsman and furniture maker. We look forward to seeing more of Darrell Peart's unique and exciting furniture designs.

WS: How and when did you decide to become a woodworker?

DP: The conscious decision to pursue woodworking as a lifelong career came in 1973 at the culmination of a hitchhiking trip from San Francisco to Seattle (and back again) Prior to this I had been feeling a bit lost. I quit my job (which was woodworking - making laminated beams) and set out to have an adventure. Along with a friend and $20 between us – we thumbed it to SF. On the way back we got a ride with a young woman who made and sold stuff at the Pike Place Market (Seattle). During the long ride home the primary topic of conservation was about being creative – making things. Within a couple of weeks of returning home, I armed myself with a saber saw, blow torch and wire brush – and started making wooden items at the Market. It all progressed from there.

WS: Growing up, who and what inspired you to follow a path in woodworking?

DP: The only direct inspiration came from my great grandfather who was a carpenter. When I was about five years old I was captivated watching him build an addition to a cabin. I especially remember him hanging a window and installing a pocket door – it fascinated me! My mother and father both inspired me – but in an indirect way regarding woodworking. My mother always wanted to be an artist. She would tell me "an artist sees the world differently". From an early age this had me thinking about art and creative ventures. My Dad was not a creative person but he was hard working and honest. He placed a high value on what he called an "honest effort". Whenever I was struggling and having a hard time – my Dad's voice was in my head – "Is this an honest effort?" It kept me going.

WS: You are a highly-regarded and prolific furniture designer, maker. What kinds of furniture do you design + make and in what style?

DP: Over the years I have designed and built just most every kind of free standing furniture Although much of my work has revolved around furniture for dining rooms, bedrooms, and executive offices. I am probably best known for my Greene & Greene style pieces. For the past few years I have been wandering a bit afar of traditional G&G. While my work certainly retains some G&G elements - I'm not sure if it can still be called Greene & Greene.

WS: Are you primarily self-taught or did you attend formal training to learn your woodworking and furniture design?

DP: When it comes to woodworking my education was what I like to call "self–directed". I had a lot of "on the job training" - having worked at several commercial shops. The variety of experiences taught me that there is no one source with all the best answers. There are multiple ways to accomplish things – and to never assume your current way is the best. Probably the most valuable thing I learned though was problem-solving. We were often given highly custom projects with no roadmap. This could be very stressful! But it taught me to think through things and find my own answers - which in turn was of immense help when I had to teach myself some aspect of woodworking. On the design side... I am 100% self-taught. I think with the right mentor I might have benefited greatly – or the wrong mentor could have done damage. I feel really good art cannot be taught "by the numbers". Design is fueled by inspiration and guided by intuition. It's something we already have that needs to be nurtured.

Photo by Darrell Peart

TERCET TABLE, 2014   MAHOGANY, EBONY, SPALTED WOOD   21" H x 25.75" W x 25.75" D

AURORA OFFICE CREDENZA, 2013   MAHOGANY, EBONY
30 1/8" H x 53" W x 23" D
Darrell Peart Seattle, WA USA

WS: Having written two books on Greene & Greene, it is safe to say you are an expert on this style of furniture. What attracted you to the Arts & Crafts movement and in particular, the Greene & Greene style of furniture?

DP: The furniture of the American Arts & Crafts Movement took joinery and treated it as a thing of beauty. Being a woodworker this had great appeal to me – to make your method of work part of the art. Greene & Greene took American Arts & Crafts to a new level. Not only was joinery celebrated but one of the big fascinations for me was this universe of detail that all related to the context as a whole.

WS: What inspired you to begin incorporating Greene & Greene elements in your furniture designs? In a few words, can you describe a few of the elements including the well-known Ebony Plugs and Cloud Lifts?

DP: I saw in G&G more than just the individual elements themselves. To me it was alive – it had DNA. This excited me like nothing else! There was all this stuff going on - even the smallest of details had a purpose – nothing was superfluous! It was this concept that a design had life really captivated me. To my way of seeing things, the ebony plugs present the illusion of strength. They steadfastly aid in holding the various parts of the structure together. There is something intrinsically satisfying about an object that is well built to withstand time and toil (this is the probably maker in me speaking). The cloud-lift often implies strength as well – but a different kind of strength. The widening of a rail next to an adjoining leg (widening caused by cloud lift) conveys the illusion of extra weight holding capacity. Sometimes a cloud–lift can be used to lighten a rail up while (making the design less "chunky") maintaining a sense of strength. OR - sometimes cloud lifts can be utilized a way to finesse a transition.

WS: It is said that you are one of the top eight furniture designers in the industry. What methodology do you follow when developing a furniture design?

DP: For my best work, I have not found a method that I can turn on and use as needed. If I have a project to put out with short notice – what I do is draw something up within the parameters given. I critique the drawing and through a process of elimination, I identify what's wrong with it. This will yield acceptable work but not my best stuff. Sometimes a design comes to me fully formed - then it's just a matter of recording it before it leaves my consciousness. Other times an idea is vague in my mind – then it's a matter of drawing and re-drawing until something clicks.

WS: An emphasis on furniture design is a large part of your furniture making. What advice do you have for woodworkers to learn this subject?

DP: The rules of design are a good starting point – but only a starting point. I view the rules as "training wheels". They were of great help in the beginning, but eventually they just hold you back from further progress. At some point the rules need to be left behind. Eventually let inspiration be the spark and intuition (which you have developed) be your guide.

WS: You practice what you call "Precision Woodworking" involving CAD drawings and precise measurements. Can you elaborate on this process?

DP: CAD allows me to produce highly accurate drawings. Measurements for cut-lists can then be produced with extreme accuracy. No longer are you relying upon full scale layouts that are limited by the thickness of a pencil line or the ability of the person at the other end of the tape to "pinch an inch" correctly. Measurements taken with calipers and indicators give you the ability to quickly cut perfect fitting joinery. In the beginning I would often cut one part then cut the next part to fit to the first part. Precision Woodworking allows me to cut most of the parts out with full confidence that it will all fit together.

KLINKER TABLE, 2017 MAHOGANY, CROTCH MAHOGANY, EBONY
17" H x 34" D   Darrell Peart Seattle, WA USA
Photo by Darrell Peart

YUKI NO HANA, 2013 MAHOGANY, EBONY, FUSED GLASS   21" H x 25" W x 25" D

WS: You have branched out into teaching woodworking and furniture making at your own school. What satisfaction does teaching new students bring to you?

DP: I get a thrill when I see the lights go on – when someone really gets a concept. I like the idea that I was a part of someone's learning process – and that learning process has a life of its own. It may well someday surpass my abilities. But it's not all a one way street with teaching. There have been several instances where I have learned from a student as well. Learning is a life-long thing. Always be open to opportunities to expand.

WS: How would you describe your current work and what inspires it?

DP: My current work is in flux. I am no longer actively seeking commission work -so I am free to peruse my whims. By nature, I like order. In my design work this translates to symmetry, balance, and a hierarchical order. But there is also a part of me that wants to rebel against it all -   In balancing these two opposing points of view – my current work always retains a hierarchical order – but chaos is sometimes at work and competes with symmetry and balance for dominance.

WS: Do you have a favorite piece? If so, which one and why?

DP: I have a couple of favorites. The 1st isn't necessarily my best work but is a sentimental favorite. My "Aurora Table Desk "was designed many years ago. It was 1st piece where 'the lights went on" - where I suddenly understood in a conscious way what I was trying to do with design. Currently my favorite piece is my "Tall Corner Table". I am excited about this piece because it is pointing the way to what's next. What's next is always the most exciting!

YUKI NO HANA GLASS, 2013 FUSED GLASS BY DOUGLAS HANSON 25" D
Darrell Peart Seattle, WA USA
Photo by Darrell Peart

WS: Which woods do prefer working with and why?

DP: If good Honduras mahogany is available (which it usually is not) – that would be a favorite. What I like about it is that it is very mellow. It allows the design to do the work. In other words it is not relying upon wild contrasts or crazy grain to float the design. Sometimes "wild and crazy" makes for some interesting chaos (which I like to interject) though. The contrast with a mellow wood such as mahogany can be powerful. (a note here – interject wild and crazy at your own risk) Since good Honduras mahogany is difficult to find these days – I often default to Sapele. Its not quite as mellow but the predictable straight lines of "ribbon" cut can be used to advantage.

WS: Are there any mediums, methods or furniture styles you have not yet explored but hope to in the future?

DP: I am not sure if there are any particular new styles I would like to explore. Occasionally I see work by some other furniture maker that appeals to me - not to copy but to use as a vague general direction.

WS: To date, what has been the most rewarding experience involving your furniture and being a furniture designer + maker?

DP: Probably no one incident – but the ongoing quest for a deeper understanding of design is most rewarding. There is an elusive quality to design work – its often a fleeting image that can be very fragile. Capturing that image and turning it into reality is ultimately satisfying and rewarding.

WS: What advice would you give to someone who is aspiring to become a woodworker and furniture designer?

DP: Find a style or particular specialty that excites you and stick with it. Your excitement will be the fuel that keeps you going. A specialty will set you apart from others and get you noticed.

WS: What are you currently working on that you would like to mention?

DP: I just finished a revised version of my Tall Corner Table. Sometimes the 1st version of a design has to sink in for a while before you can revisit it and revise it. It's at the finisher now – can't wait to get it back!

WS: Are there any upcoming projects, books and/or events that you would like to mention?

DP: I am currently trying to clear my schedule so I can work on a furniture design book. I have been thinking about this for years. I still have some outstanding commitments – but I hope to get started here in a few months.

Photo by Richard McNamee

FREMONT NIGHTSTAND, 2010 MAHOGANY, EBONY   27" H x 26" W x 18" D
Darrell Peart Seattle, WA USA

SOCIAL MEDIA
SPREAD THE WORD

by Norman Pirollo

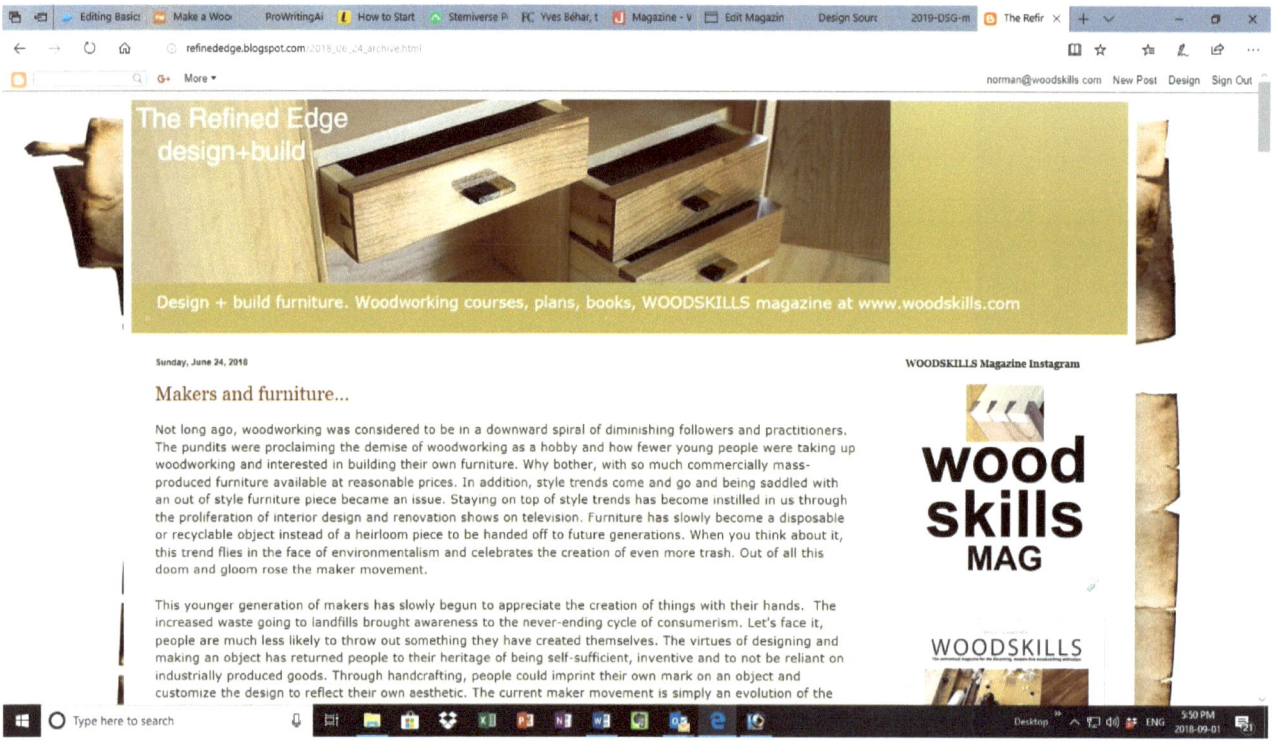

Snapshot of The Refined Edge blog which chronicles my journey into furniture making. This blog was established in 2007 where I continue to blog with a large following.

A woodworker with many years of experience may have come to terms with the direction they wish to follow. In many cases, they embrace a quieter, less hurried form of woodworking. Their woodworking passion is better served in the enjoyment of creating a piece rather than simply achieving the end goal. Instead, somebody just starting out will perhaps wonder why today they should be performing manual tasks such as hand planing, hand sawing boards and creating joinery by hand. After all, isn't this why machinery was created, to facilitate the processing of boards used in furniture making? Hasn't the trend in industry always been to make our jobs easier and more productive? This is the dilemma facing many woodworkers today, specifically new woodworkers. I don't pretend to have a solution and can only form an opinion through many years of experience in both camps. As a former hi-tech person and convert to a quieter form of woodworking, I would much rather work with traditional, time-proven methods than to embrace the latest in machinery whose goal is to make my life easier. I too faced this dilemma and have been minimizing the use of machinery in my woodworking. In the process, I have since learned to appreciate wood as a medium and not just to use it as a means to an end. The machines I use today are effectively motorized hand tools, nothing sophisticated. This is where I draw the line.

Internet Marketing

Only a few years ago, advertising and marketing were performed through traditional mediums such as magazine ads, newspaper ads, and the ubiquitous Yellow Pages. Today, the Internet makes several online marketing resources available. It makes complete sense to have an Internet presence for the woodworking business you are developing. A large part of an Internet presence is in the form of a website. A website can display a gallery of your furniture and includes sections devoted to your biography, work philosophy, genre and style of furniture, and an optional blog. Other website components include contact information, general inquiries, and purchasing and commissioning information for clients.

My web presence has been available since 1996, originally offered through third party online gallery websites. A woodworking and furniture related website devoted exclusively to my work was developed and launched in 1997. Websites of this era were primitive as website software was evolving and had not been perfected or standardized. Internet bandwidth was low, speeds were low, and overall visual quality and resolution were dismal.

In this period, digital photography was also in its infancy. Digital photography has simplified the photographing of furniture pieces to make the images available online. Today, website software quality and variety have dramatically increased, costs have come down, and there are many skilled individuals available to create your website. Internet bandwidth has increased an order of magnitude in the intervening twenty years with photo and video resolution increasing accordingly. Having witnessed this evolution, it is much more pleasant to create, update, and market a website today.

Web sites work hand in hand with social media in bringing awareness to your woodworking business and furniture making. Digital photography technology has also progressed exponentially over this period, and costs have dropped considerably. Website hosting fees are very reasonable today. All this makes it much more appealing and affordable to have a website today. Another factor to consider is that your competition likely has a web presence, so it is necessary to publish your own website to remain competitive. Today, it is expected for a furniture maker to have a dedicated website with info about their business, philosophy and a gallery of their work. A blog is also critical to marketing yourself as a furniture maker.

Snapshot of website homepage
[Pirollo Design]

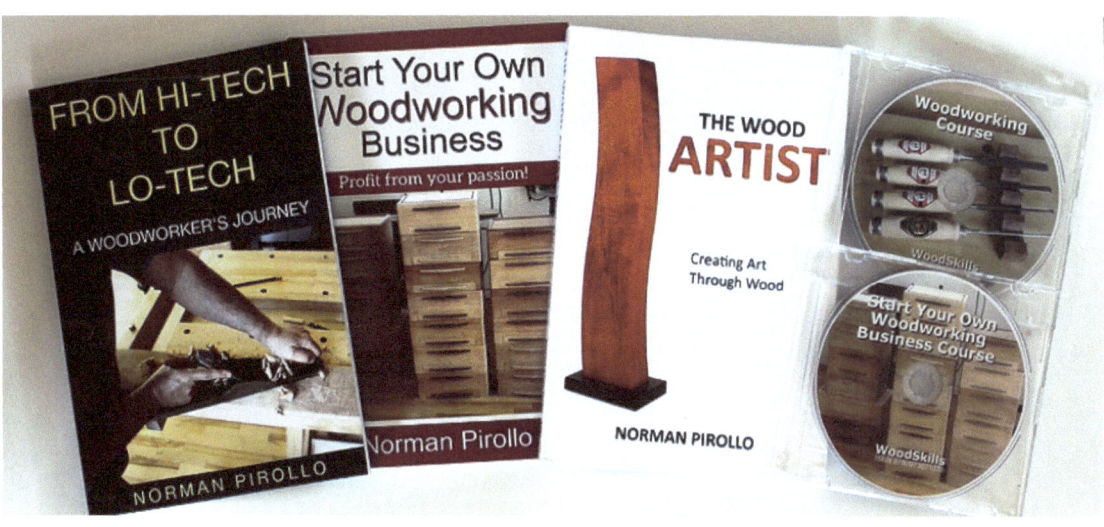

Website developers can be easily found in most cities and you should shop for both the best price and quality of website you have designed. It is necessary to add that ongoing maintenance costs of hosting and updating a website need to be factored in to the initial cost of creating and publishing a website. You can also design and create your own website. Today, several website hosting companies are available that enable you to create your own website and have it hosted. Templates are typically used to perform this and the results are good. Having used such a process recently, I was impressed at the quality and ease of creating a website.

Photographing the furniture you create is an important criteria in your marketing. Some furniture makers perform their own photography while others hire professional photographers to regularly drop in and photograph their work. If you opt to perform your own photography, you will need to invest in considerable photographic equipment. Vital equipment includes a tripod, a large backdrop; auxiliary lighting and a high quality DSLR type camera. It will be necessary to take workshops to work a camera and perform studio photography. An advantage to shooting your own work is the flexibility it provides.

You can photograph the work at your leisure instead of waiting on a professional photographer. Today, I combine my photography with that of professional photographers. If a piece of furniture can not be easily photographed, I do not hesitate to contact a professional photographer for the task. It is well worth it since my time is valuable and outstanding photography can make a commission or sale. The takeaway is to not always take the most inexpensive path in your marketing. Better quality marketing often leads to sales which more than compensate for the extra cost of the marketing tool, be it photography or advertising.

In recent years, there has been an explosion of social media platforms that can bring awareness to your furniture making business. The most popular and widespread platforms include Twitter, Facebook, Instagram, Linkedin and YouTube. The following paragraphs describe the social media platforms I use most often, and those that have the greatest potential for exposure of your business. Consequently, I have embraced social media as an effective marketing tool for business.

Snapshot of website gallery [Pirollo Design]

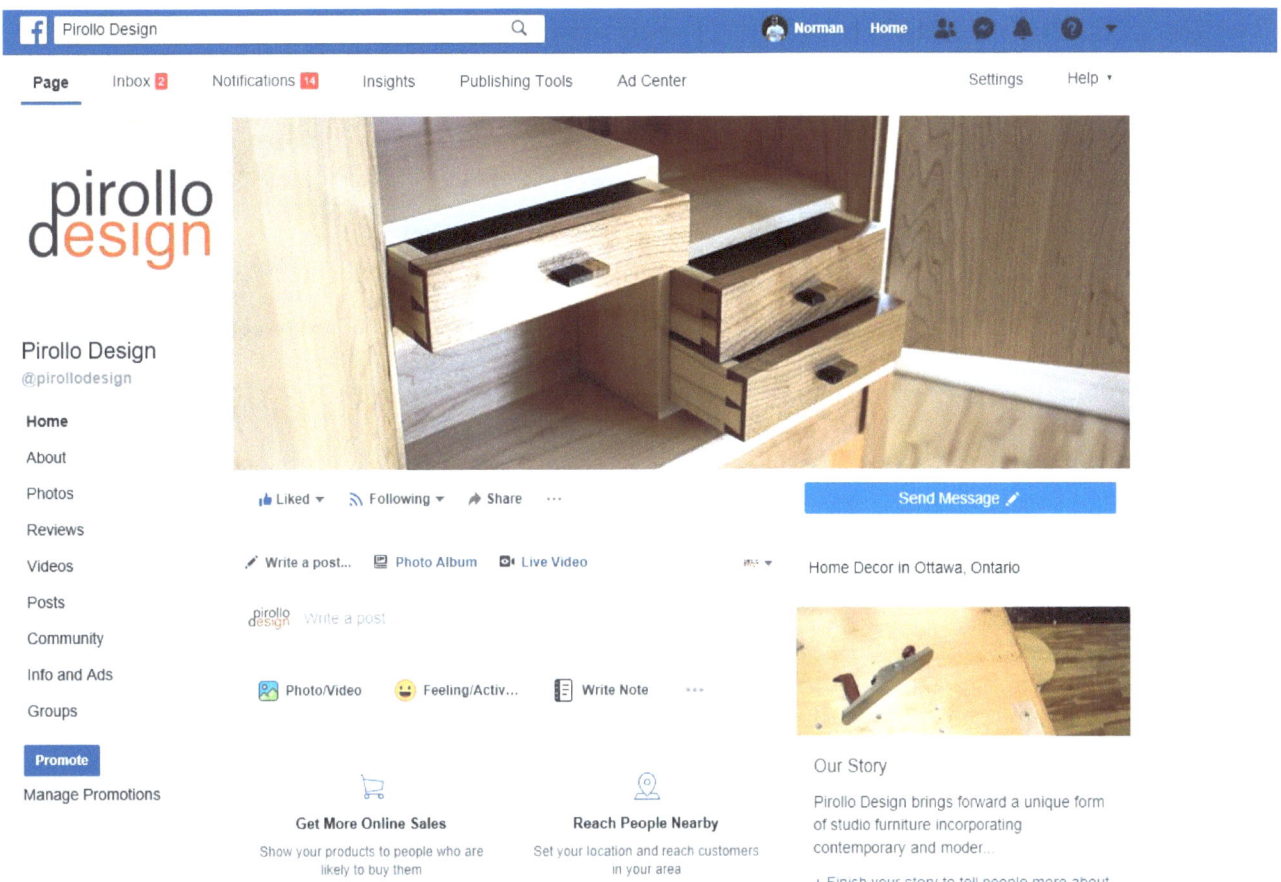

Snapshot of a Facebook Business page [Pirollo Design]

The original social media platform, **Facebook**, has evolved to include an option specifically to promote business. The Facebook Page option is designed with business in mind. A Facebook Business page is separate from your Personal page but is easily accessed through your Facebook profile. For example, a personal user on Facebook can create a business page and have it available to view while logged into Facebook. This significantly reduces the steps necessary to access and update your Business page. It is relatively straightforward to create a Facebook Business page and populate it with critical business information.

The Business page then takes on a life of its own and with clever marketing will draw clients to your business. Facebook Business pages are also used as a peer-to-peer networking tool to discover other businesses to aid in marketing your business. I call this cross-pollination. Other businesses, local and distant, will find and seek you for business-to-business activity. Posts on a Facebook Business page include new product announcements, new furniture designs, shop additions, and positive reviews.

Static information on a Facebook Business page includes your business location, business hours, a website link, contact info, and specific information for your business. A feature a business account provides is advertising in the form of promotional post boosts and dedicated ad campaigns. Facebook ad campaigns are set up to target the demographic most likely to purchase your work. The ads are in-line with regular posts when people scroll through their news feed. If targeting and focused interests have been strategically set up in a Facebook ad campaign, the likelihood of a response to your ad increases.

Ad campaigns can be set up as either CPC (Cost Per Click) or Post views. The CPC strategy directs a person to your website or wherever your work is sold. Post views instead present your post to as many viewers as possible, ideal for branding of your furniture designs. In optimal circumstances, your Facebook post will be shared by a Facebook viewer. Sharing compounds post visibility and is invaluable to getting the word out of your woodworking business or furniture making.

Twitter is another of the wave of new social media platforms that can expose your business to tens of thousands of potential clients. By regularly posting and engaging with other Twitter businesses and followers, your posts will be seen by significantly more people. Being active is key to being successful on any of these social media platforms. Twitter is historically one of the earliest social media platforms and has grown to a large membership. Twitter users engage with each other. It is possible to join Twitter on a personal basis or set yourself up as a business. A business account provides the most benefit to your business. A Twitter business account can tap into hundreds of thousands of people with similar interests. Each instance of a Twitter post acquires Likes, Comments and Retweets which increase engagement of your post and raise its ranking. Through an advanced algorithm, a higher ranking Twitter post is then served to more followers. It is this cascading exposure that will benefit your business.

Twitter posts include text with static images or a video. Hashtags included in your Twitter post strategically target certain niches. Hashtags have a life of their own and facilitate a search for a category of post. For example, an often-used hashtag applied to my posts on all social media platforms is #woodworking. This hashtag increases the possibility of being seen by a Twitter user using the search term woodworking. Another feature of a Twitter business account is advertising. Twitter ad campaigns can be set up to target the demographic most likely to purchase your work. The ads are in-line with regular posts when people scroll through their news feeds. If the targeting is correct and focused interests have been set up in an ad campaign, likelihood of a response to the ad increases.

Ad campaigns can be set up with either PPC (Pay Per Click) or Tweet engagement, Video views, App downloads or to simply increase your followers. The PPC strategy drives traffic to your website or wherever your work is sold. A tweet engagement presents your post to as many viewers as possible and increases brand awareness. In a Twitter ad campaign, you set a daily budget and duration of the campaign. The ad campaign runs continually until the expiry date.

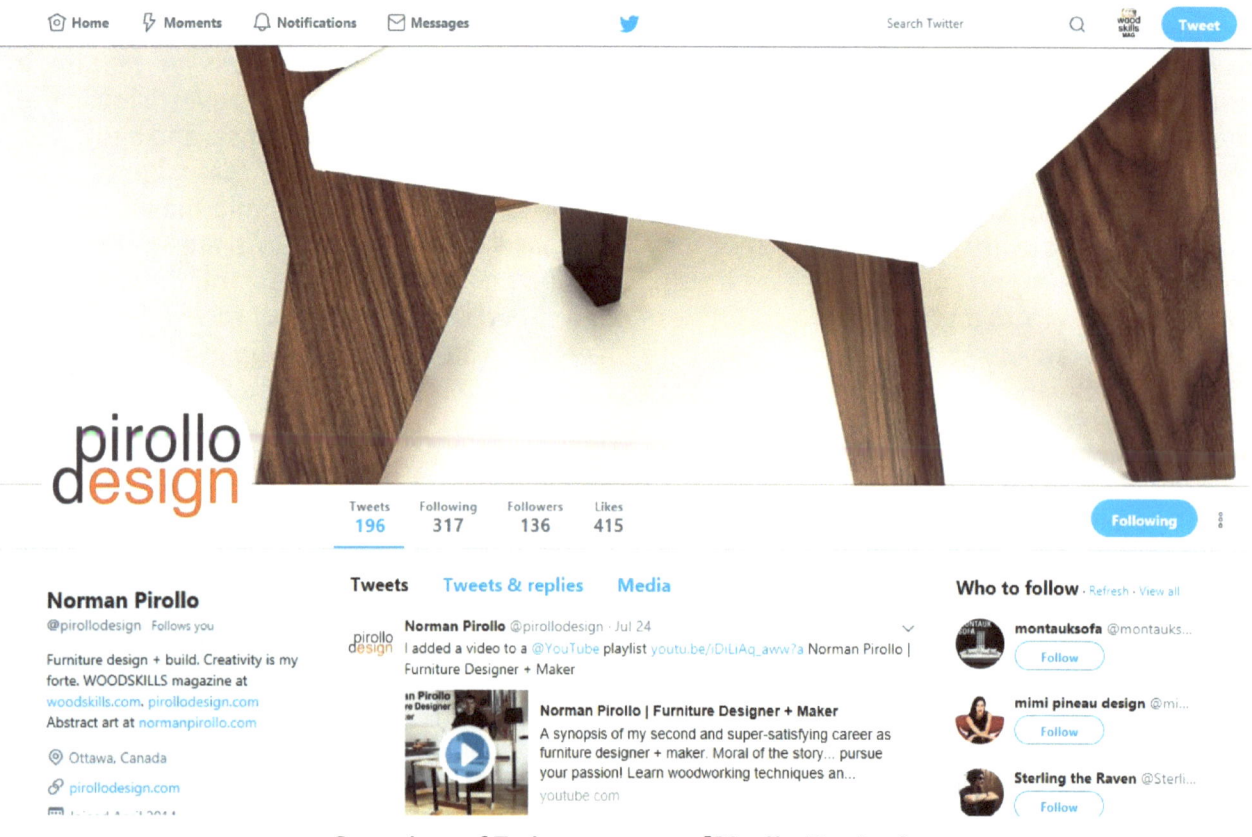

Snapshot of Twitter account [Pirollo Design]

Detailed Twitter analytics are available to monitor response to your ad. Monetization and affiliate marketing are features of social media platforms such as Twitter. A large number of people tap into the monetization of Twitter and the recurring money gained from widespread exposure and engagement of their posts. An ideal monetization situation is when a Twitter user clicks a link to your website and makes a purchase. However, maintaining a social media effort will take valuable time away from your business. You need to determine how much of your time to allocate to social media so the impact to your core business is minimal. Also important is the return on investment of a social media ad campaign. If insufficient results are received, it is necessary to either modify the campaign or seek alternate forms of advertising.

Linkedin was an early social media adopter on the Internet. It is the most professional and business oriented of the social media platforms. A presence on Linkedin is almost expected of a business or career professional today. Linkedin is used mainly for professional networking among its members. Career professionals can share their successes, seek new opportunities and make it known they are in the market for new career challenges. Linkedin also caters to businesses and has become an excellent platform to make announcements or introduce new products. Although it is not expected for individuals or businesses to post on Linkedin as regularly as other social media platforms, the weighting and value of each post is substantially more effective. Consequently, the quality of posts on Linkedin is greater than on other social media platforms.

Linkedin membership is freely available, although the method of creating and building your social network differs somewhat from other platforms. To become a Linkedin member, you create a profile which includes relevant information including your bio, CV, accomplishments, education. As well, your current and past employment is noted. As a furniture maker, this is where you indicate you are self-employed at your own furniture making business. Once you are a Linkedin member, the Linkedin concept is to request that other members join your social network and form a connection with you. This concept applies to both individuals and businesses.

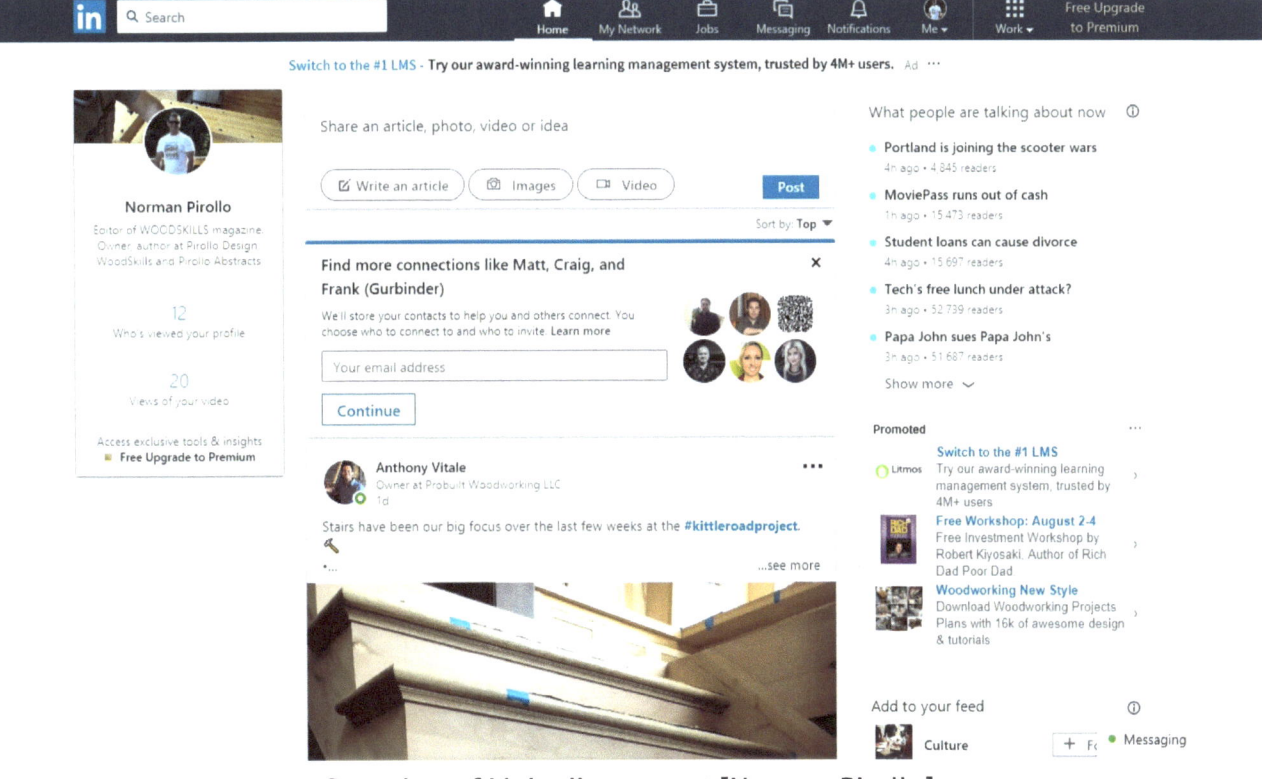

Snapshot of Linkedin account [Norman Pirollo]

There are nested levels of participation in your social network with each person in your network considered a connection. Your network comprises 1st degree, 2nd degree, and 3rd degree connections. A higher ranking or 1st degree indicates a close connection to an individual and you have invited or have been invited into your respective networks. A 2nd degree connection is a member connected to your 1st degree connection. A 3rd degree individual has a connection with your 2nd degree connection. This concept allows you to cultivate relationships with other Linkedin members that have a vested interest in your type of business. Rather than simply acquiring followers as on other social media platforms, Linkedin prefers you select and nurture a relationship with a smaller but more relevant community of members. The Linkedin emphasis is on quality of contacts rather than sheer numbers of followers. Since Linkedin focuses on professionalism, the posts are centered on successes, careers, business opportunities, new product launches, awards and recognition.

As a furniture maker, Linkedin is an ideal medium to share a new furniture design or woodworking product. Individual users on Linkedin can follow businesses and companies. Linkedin also has groups of which you can join or even create. As a member of a Linkedin group, you and your business will be in even closer proximity to prospective clients. As a furniture maker, Linkedin enables you to develop a substantial network of people interested in your work and acquiring it. Business opportunities can be created and developed through Linkedin. Nurturing relationships with other businesses can assist with outsourcing certain processes or components of your furniture. For example, several furniture makers would rather not finish their furniture pieces and instead outsource to professional finishers. Another example is if you combine metal and wood in your furniture, you can seek other businesses to outsource the fabrication of the metal components. Other businesses can also seek you out to create furniture or furniture related opportunities.

Instagram is a relatively new kid on the social media block. Instagram began as a photo sharing platform and still is. At the time of this writing, Instagram has also largely embraced video. Video posts in the form of stories of varying durations can now be posted. The duration is limited to seconds or a few minutes, but stories are very effective at engaging viewers. You can demonstrate a new technique or process. The traditional post with only images continues to form a large percentage of Instagram posts and is extremely effective at increasing the number of people or followers to your account. This effectively increases your exposure as a furniture maker.

Instagram accounts used to be strictly personal although the recent addition of a business account option has changed this. It is now possible to convert a personal account to a business account. Instagram business accounts have the advantage of providing analytics to the account owner. Through analytics, the engagement and exposure a post receives can be viewed in the form of charts and figures.

Analytics is a valuable tool for a business owner. A business owner can determine the demographic viewing and engaging with their posts, at what times of day and the weekdays their posts are most active. Through regular posting and engagement with your Instagram followers and other Instagram accounts, more people see your posts and the posts move up in ranking. Being active is the key to success on any social media platform. Instagram is a relative newcomer to social media but has grown exponentially in the past few years. Each Instagram post acquires Likes, Comments and Shares. Each of these increase engagement of the post and raise its ranking.

A highly ranked Instagram post is served to even more followers. It is this cascading exposure that benefits a business the most. Another feature a business account provides is advertising. Instagram ad campaigns are a recent addition and are set up to target the demographic most likely to purchase your work. The ads are in-line with regular posts when people scroll through their feeds.

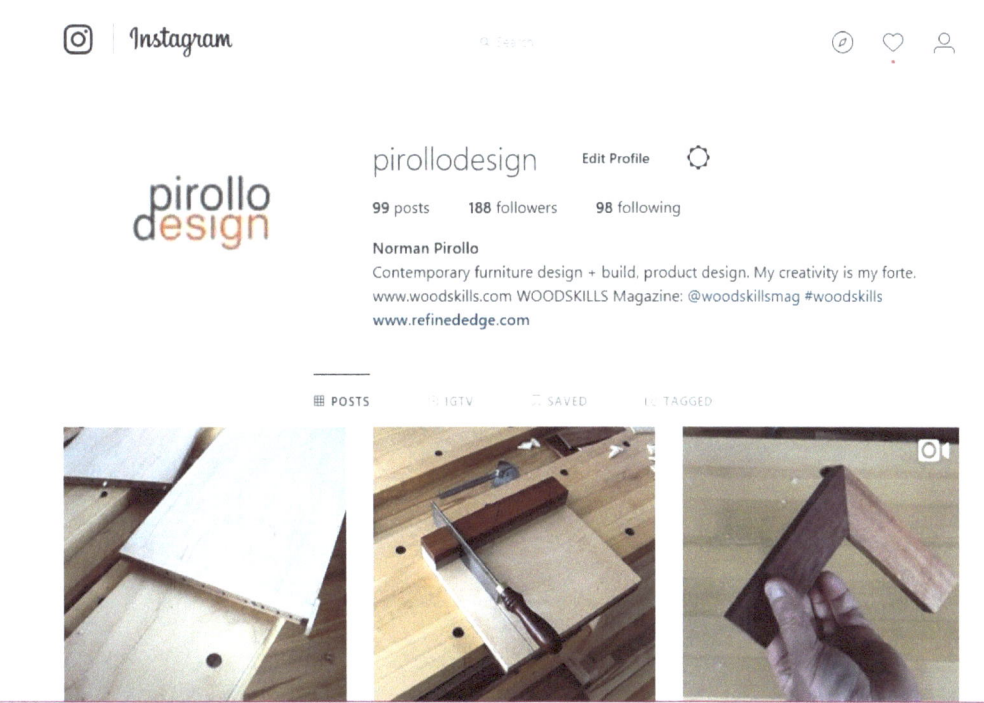

Snapshot of Instagram account [Pirollo Design]

If the Instagram targeting is correct and focused interests have been set up in an ad campaign, the likelihood of response to the Instagram ad increases. Ad campaigns can be set up as either PPC (Pay Per Click) or a post engagement, Video view, App download or to increase your followers. The PPC strategy drives traffic to your website or wherever your work is sold. Post engagement instead presents your post to as many viewers as possible, increasing the exposure you receive and branding of your product. As of this writing, Instagram does not offer monetization, although it will be offered soon according to industry insiders. Posting and reading posts consumes an inordinate amount of time which is valuable time away from your business. You will need to determine how much of your time to allocate to social media, so it does not significantly interfere with your core furniture making business.

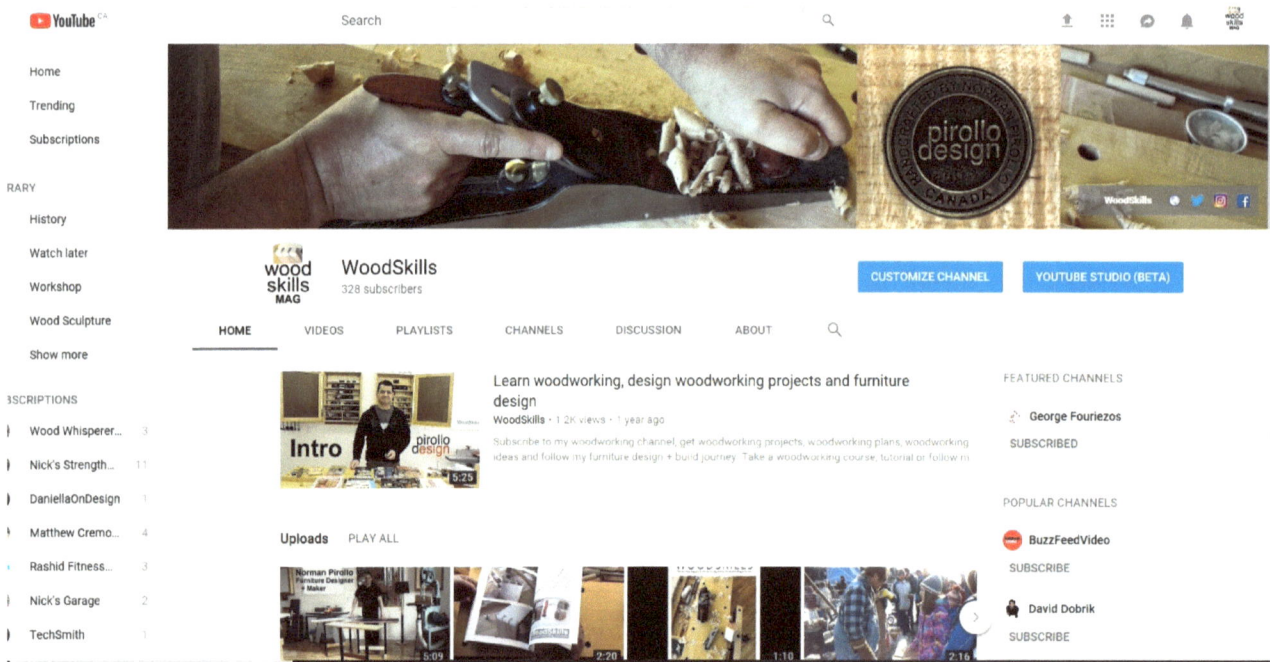

Snapshot of YouTube account [WoodSkills]

YouTube is another popular social media platform to promote your business and develop a following. The premise of YouTube is the sharing of videos. It is the oldest large-scale video sharing service available on the Internet. Millions of members and viewers connect with YouTube daily. A member can create an account and a channel associated with it. The channel should have a unique, easily remembered name. The channel is then populated with videos the member creates. YouTube is ubiquitous and widely recognized as the go to source for instructional videos on wide-ranging topics. The caveat to Youtube's popularity is that videos are mostly home spun. There is considerable chaff to sort through to find video gems. If one needs to quickly learn about a particular topic or product, YouTube is a good choice for a video explaining the topic.

YouTube is a large and well-known platform for sharing videos but not so much for developing business relationships. As a furniture maker, YouTube offers the potential to demonstrate your furniture making techniques. YouTube is also an effective platform to host videos describing the furniture pieces you intend to market. As well, you can profile yourself as a furniture maker and promote your business through YouTube. I regularly post videos on my YouTube channel of various techniques used in my furniture making studio. Through YouTube videos, you can describe the joinery you use, your philosophy of furniture making, and the processes you follow to create furniture.

Proficiency in creating videos is a criteria although with the current crop of software, this is becoming simpler. With basic editing, videos can today be created on smartphones and transferred directly to YouTube. The choice is yours whether you wish to create videos that are professional in appearance or post videos as you go. The latter choice is often the best choice since video editing can be time consuming. This is valuable time away from your core business. My advice is to maintain video quality but make editing simple so it does not interfere with your work. Once your YouTube channel is established, you can also create playlists of videos. This feature allows you to organized videos by topic. Playlists make it easier for a viewer of your channel to select the relevant videos they choose to watch. The YouTube platform also has a highly regarded search feature to search through the mammoth YouTube repository of videos on almost any subject or topic.

Apply optimal keywords to your videos and the search function enables a viewer to find your videos. YouTube viewers can also comment on videos, allowing you to engage with viewers and increases the exposure your video receives. Videos can also be shared among viewers. Through sharing, the potential for your video to be viewed increases substantially. If a viewer likes your videos and channel, they have the option to subscribe to the channel. Whenever you post a video to your channel, subscribers are automatically notified of the latest video. Views to your videos and channel increase by having the number of subscribers to your channel increase. The monetization option does exist on the YouTube platform. Once your subscriber number surpasses a certain mark, namely 100k, you have the potential of earning money through your videos. This is in the form of compensation of number of views per video. The takeaway is to embrace social media and use it to market and publicize your business.

Norman Pirollo
Custom Furniture
www.pirollodesign.com
Instagram: @pirollodesign

WOOD FIGURE
HOW TO READ

Discussion of how to identify wood figure and adapt it to a furniture design. When wood figure and wood graphics are embraced in a furniture design, harmony and a calm aesthetic are introduced to the piece.

by Norman Pirollo

The visual appeal of wood is determined by its color, texture and grain orientation. Grain orientation is the pattern of grain visible on the wood surface. Grain is characterized through use of the term wood graphics. Grain orientation differs between species of wood. How the wood was cut from a tree can also affect grain orientation. Experienced sawyers are familiar with several methods of sawing logs into boards where each method provides a different grain pattern. Each method also determines the dimensional stability of a sawn board.

As an example, a plain-sawn board cut from a log exhibits the most pronounced grain pattern in the form of a cathedral pattern. This method of sawing logs is the most efficient, economical and timesaving for sawyers. The cathedral grain pattern, however, is not well-suited to fine furniture construction. It is difficult to orient boards with a cathedral pattern and not have the grain pattern visually clash throughout a piece of furniture. Plain-sawn boards are also recognized as not being dimensionally stable. Plain-sawn boards are prone to cupping along their width, due to the boards cut at a tangent or tangentially to the growth rings.

Plain-sawn boards with cathedral pattern are commonly used in the door panels of a frame and panel assembly. To achieve the different wood patterns or graphics, wood logs need to be cut a certain way. Defined and standardized cutting processes have been established to produce boards with common grain characteristics.

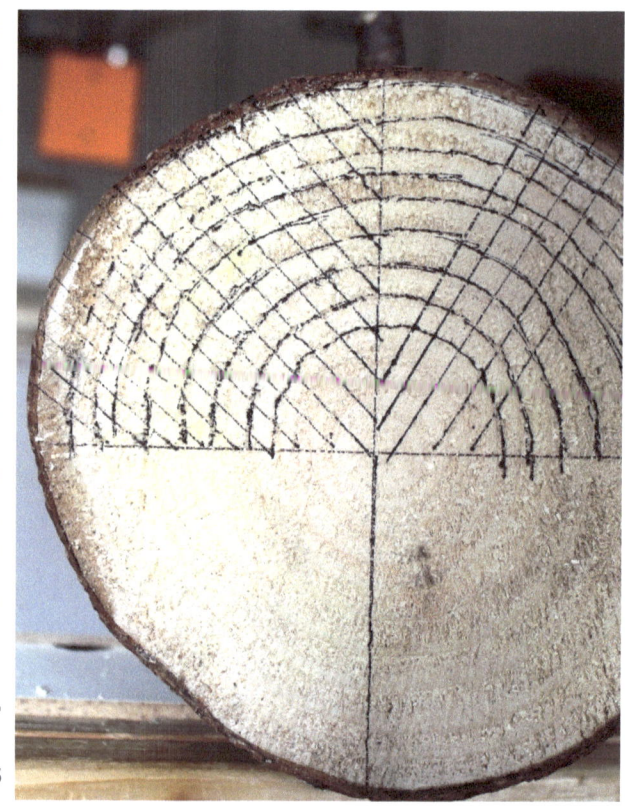

Plain-sawn wood features a pronounced cathedral grain pattern or graphics due to the board being sawn through and through from a log. Boards of logs cut parallel to the grain orientation and tangent to growth rings of the tree exhibit plain-sawn grain. The sawn board also includes the heartwood and the sapwood areas. Each of these areas has grain oriented differently.

To achieve a linear visual aesthetic in a wood pattern or wood graphic, boards need to be cut from a log using a different method. The most common alternative cuts are rift-sawn and quarter-sawn. Boards of logs cut parallel to the direction of the grain but also sliced perpendicularly through the radius of the growth rings exhibit quarter-sawn grain.

**Log divided into quarters.
End of log marked for quarter-sawn cuts.
Boards are perpendicular to growth rings**

Rift-sawn and quarter-sawn methods minimize the exaggerated cathedral wood graphics of plain-sawn boards. The resulting grain pattern or wood graphic is linear and displays convex or concave curves when viewed longitudinally. The curved pattern or graphic creates harmony in the visual aesthetic of door frame members or in case construction. Often, a linear grain orientation is better suited for certain components of a furniture piece. A linear grain pattern is ideal for structural members of a table, stand, case or in the rails and stiles of a frame and panel assembly. The nondescript linear grain facilitates assembly of the members of a furniture piece.

A linear pattern or graphic is not as visually distracting as a cathedral pattern. Wood grain patterns or graphics can also be affected by the growing conditions of a tree or how a tree grows. The term reaction wood is used to describe a tree that has not grown straight and true but instead grown in a stressful environment. The stress can include constant high winds, the tree growing on the sloped side of a hill, or the tree was damaged and grew in a compromised direction. Reaction wood is identifiable by its unusual grain orientation. The grain pattern is neither straight nor cathedral.

Plain-sawn board face with pronounced cathedral grain pattern

Instead, the grain exhibits an irregular pattern. Boards cut from reaction wood logs are usually avoided in furniture construction due to inherent tension and instability in the wood. Wood tension can manifest itself in different ways, all unfavorable to furniture making. A squirrely reaction wood pattern and pent-up tension creates boards that are unstable and likely to move irregularly or split. Highly unstable reaction wood can be detrimental when used in a furniture project. However, it can be advantageous when a certain aesthetic or visual characteristic is desired. Reaction wood often has a unique, exciting grain pattern that can be a design element in a furniture piece. Reaction wood can be used as a sculpture base or used as an element in a sculpture. Diseased or injured wood is also associated with unique wood grain characteristics or wood graphics. Disease can be in the form of the residue of bugs which have infiltrated a log.

WOOD FIGURE
HOW TO READ

The bugs often leave a colored trail. Wood exhibiting this characteristic is considered spalted. Ambrosia maple comes to mind as an excellent example of diseased or spalted wood. Ambrosia beetles leave black streaks behind that highlight the grain pattern of a board. This distinguishing effect can be a design element in a furniture piece. Injured woods such as Bird's Eye Maple, Burl Wood, Curly Maple, Quilted Maple and Flame Birch also exhibit exciting wood grain characteristics. The suspicion is that these unique wood grain characteristics are due to injury. There exist several schools of thought explaining why the wood exhibits unique grain characteristics.

Collectively, the unique grain characteristics found in figured wood are recognized as elements. The term figured wood describes wood exhibiting an unusual grain pattern and features that distinguish it from other wood of the same species. Figured woods form a small percentage of the typical yield of a common wood. As an example, maple trees exhibiting Bird's Eye characteristics are uncommon. Experienced loggers can sometimes identify trees exhibiting figure or flawed wood, but this is rarely the case. In most cases, a stand of trees is harvested and the lone tree with figure is then isolated after removing its bark. The tree with conspicuous wood figure is then set aside and marketed to buyers of figured woods.

Ambrosia maple board with spalted surface and colored bug trail

Highly-figured Bird's Eye Maple board exhibiting dense bird's eye figure

In isolated cases, a tree with figure is processed the same as other trees in the stand where it originated. Boards from this tree are then sold through the same distribution channels as other non-figured boards. The following describes an experience of purchasing boards from a commercial outfit. While perusing maple boards at a home center, one board stood out as being highly figured. The maple board had a rich curl figure. The board was purchased at the same price as other boards of the same species and used as veneers in door panels of my furniture. Commercial lumber mills are not set up to extract boards with unusual figure. It is cost prohibitive for a mill to set up a process to isolate these logs and resulting boards. In a commercial lumber mill, figured logs are processed similarly to other logs.

Clients seeking processed boards typically purchase wood for the species characteristics and are not seeking highly figured variants of boards. I was in the right place at the right time to find this gem of a board! Another variant in wood surfaces is alternating dark and light areas that are a result of different wood densities. This characteristic causes stain or finish to be absorbed differently along the surface. The result is considered blotchy wood. However, when viewed through an artistic eye the blotchiness yields a different result. Wood with this blotchy characteristic, when infused with transparent dye, exhibits an exciting color pattern. Color gradients of dye applied to the wood surface create a random colored and abstract surface.

Highly figured woods are prized by musical instrument makers. Figured woods are used in the fronts and backs of certain instruments. The more pronounced the figure, the higher the desirability of the board. However, highly figured logs are most often sliced into commercial veneers. The cost effectiveness of slicing multiple sheets of veneers from a log far outweigh the alternative of sawing thick boards from the same figured log. Availability of highly figured woods is often sporadic. Retailers or distributors that specialize in unusually figured woods are few. Retailers of figured woods can be found in and around major urban centers. With online retail, figured woods or veneers purchases are easier today. Most wood retailers specializing in exotic and figured woods will process and ship online orders. In the past, I have traveled to other cities to purchase figured woods. Today, although a variety of figured woods can be locally purchased, I order online when necessary. A collection of highly figured woods is always available in my wood storage. The figured woods are in the form of either sliced veneers or boards. The boards are sliced into shop-sawn veneers which are then applied to a substrate.

This is the most cost effective and efficient use of highly figured woods. Veneered panels using shop-sawn veneers are often indistinguishable from solid board variants of the same figured woods. Highly figured wood are very expensive although this depends on the amount and quality of the figure. The species of wood is also a criteria in determining the price of figured wood. Figured woods are not limited to domestic wood species. Figure is often found in exotic wood species. When out shopping for wood, I often peruse the figured wood section of a wood retailer to determine if a figured wood board appeals to me. If so, there is no hesitation in purchasing it. In all likelihood, it will likely be sold to another buyer before my next visit. Figured domestic and exotic woods are ideal to purchase and store since they have no expiry date and will never be obsolete!

Over time, I incorporated figured woods into my furniture pieces. It is critical to use figured woods judiciously in a furniture design. Although I have created display cabinets with a large proportion of figured woods, it is wise to limit the use of figured woods in your designs. The use of figured woods was expanded in my furniture pieces only after understanding the characteristics of veneered panels. A best practice is to limit the use of veneered figured wood panels, to either a frame and panel or the complete panel of a door.

It is highly advised to only use a single species of figured wood throughout. Otherwise, a distracting, visual clash will occur. Judicious use of figured woods in a furniture piece is recommended as a best practice. Too much of a good thing can destroy the intended aesthetic. In my work, application of figured woods created a new direction.

Highly-figured Bird's Eye Maple board exhibiting dense bird's eye figure

I am often on the lookout at wood retailers for highly figured boards that could be resawn into thin veneers. The dimensional stability of using veneers and more specifically, highly figured ones, was very appealing. Although sawing and preparing thin veneers from thick boards is slow and time consuming, it is a cost-effective process. Often, the board is unique in characteristics and the greater yield allows more of the board to be used. Extracting the maximum number of veneer slices from a single board is also critical in avoiding discontinuity of wood graphics. The sequential veneer slices originating from a board are considered a flitch of veneers.

Ovoid-shaped side table with highly-figured Tiger Maple top.
The exciting figure draws the eye into the unique design.

Each board of figured wood has slightly different characteristics from another board of the same species. Continuity between slices is achieved through a method of resawing slices to form a flitch. This ensures that the grain pattern or figure is matching. Veneer slices from the flitch are then slip-matched together. Grain matching is an important criterion in furniture making. There is considerably less clash in wood graphics when using this approach. Book-matching is another method of joining figured wood veneer slices. In book-matching, the slices are joined at their common edge. The pattern then becomes a mirror image on both sides of the veneer sheet. Using these methods of combining wood slices into a veneer sheet, many possibilities are available of using figured wood veneers in a furniture piece.

Having resawn a considerable amount of boards into veneers, I plan the number of slices necessary and seek boards from which to acquire the slices. The slices often need to be combined into wider sheets for the sides of cabinets. In the case of wide sheets, two slices are necessary. The use of figured woods can introduce a new dimension to your furniture designs. No longer does furniture need to be uniform in grain and consistent in appearance. Figured woods enhance the appeal of furniture. The focal point often shifts to the figured wood instead of the overall design and this needs to be factored in. Figured woods could be interpreted as nature's own abstract wood art. Furniture incorporating figured wood can be viewed as a form of art. I consider this furniture purely functional but exhibiting elements of art.

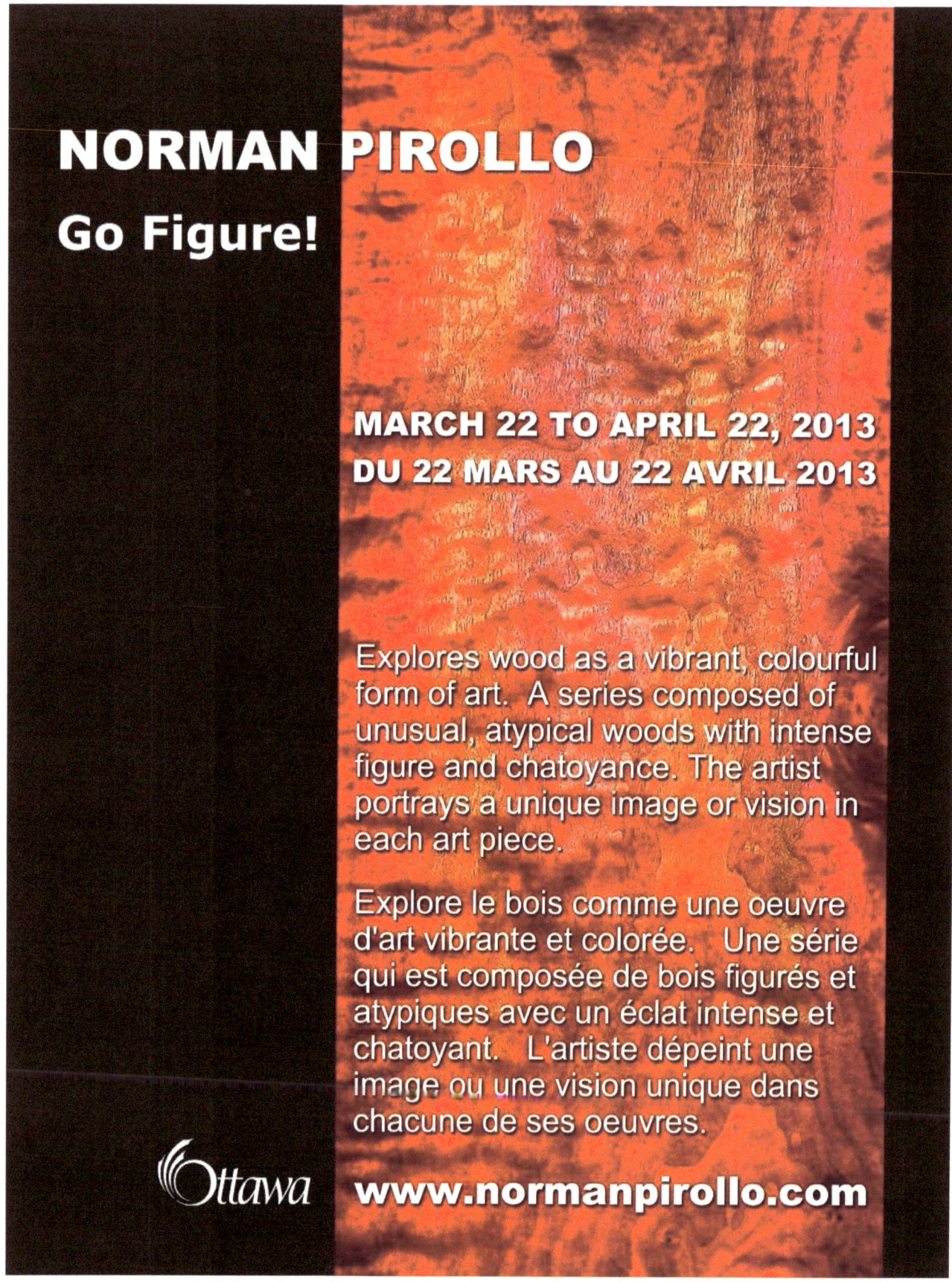

A wood art exhibition focusing on several species of wood with exciting figure and wood graphics. The exhibition centered on wood figure and graphics being a form of art. Color was infused into to the wood art pieces to pop the grain and figure.
April 2013

9824 30th Ave SW
Seattle, WA 98126

425 277 4070
www.furnituremaker.com
IG: @darrell.peart
Twitter: @DarrellPeart

WoodSkills
Instructional woodworking courseware

CLOSING THOUGHTS
by Editorial Team

This will be the end of Issue 02 of WOODSKILLS magazine. We sincerely hope the new format and contents of the magazine have provided insight to the furniture maker's featured in this issue and provide you reason to return for the next issue.

It is the objective of the editorial team at WOODSKILLS to have provided you an enjoyable woodworking experience with Issue 02. Having been exposed to countless magazines over decades, we collectively discovered a niche for a different genre of woodworking magazine. A magazine with a focus on the reasons behind a furniture design. Instead of detailed furniture construction steps, WOODSKILLS delves into the thought process behind a furniture design. As well, we describe how specific techniques and processes will advance you as a woodworker and furniture maker. The emphasis of this magazine is hand tool use, where machines can be used in the initial phase of a furniture build to prepare blanks from rough sawn timbers. Well-researched time and labor-saving precision hand tool techniques are put forward and discussed in every issue. We are not averse to the use of machines where it makes the most sense. It is wiser to emphasize hand tool use in the latter stages of a furniture build where meticulous attention to detail is necessary and preferred.

An analogy is that of a long-distance runner who maintains a steady pace early on and later sprints to the finish. Homage is paid to classic techniques such as dovetail joinery, mortise and tenon joinery, and time-proven hand tool methods. It is our belief that traditional furniture construction methods and processes should be maintained and passed on to future generations. As testament to their reliability and longevity, traditional methods have evolved little over the centuries. As well as the traditional, we put forward modern techniques and processes that make your furniture designs stand out and be unique. Our focus is one of a kind furniture, the unique furniture and wood objects that separate their makers from every other maker. Each issue includes profiles and candid conversations with established furniture designers and makers. Find out what they are passionate about, what drives them and where they draw inspiration. Often, reading about a furniture maker instills in us the enthusiasm and impetus to break through and move forward. It is not so much how but the why behind the process that is often critical in a furniture maker's mind and practice.

Inside Back Cover
KLINKER YARD GATE, 2016
SPANISH CEDAR, ART GLASS, HARDWARE
67" H x 48" W
Darrell Peart Seattle, WA USA

Outside Back Cover
WISTERIA CABINET, 2017
HONDURAN MAHOGANY, MAPLE BURL,
AMBOYNA BURL, WALNUT BURL, WALNUT,
SYCAMORE, OLIVE ASH, MARQUETRY WOODS
70" H x 36" W x 20" D
Craig Thibodeau San Diego, CA USA

Photo by Darrell Peart

Photo by Craig Carlson

www.ingramcontent.com/pod-product-compliance
Lightning Source LLC
Chambersburg PA
CBHW042031150426
43200CB00002B/18